HOW TO KNOW IF YOU'RE REALLY

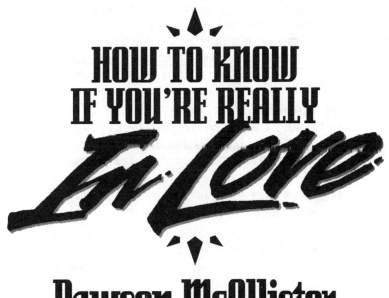

HOW TO KNOW IF YOU'RE REALLY In Love

Dawson McAllister

WORD PUBLISHING
Dallas·London·Vancouver·Melbourne

Unless otherwise indicated, Scripture quotations are from The Holy Bible, New Century Version, copyright © 1991 by Word Publishing, Dallas, Texas 75039. All rights reserved.

Other Scripture verses are from the following sources:

> The New American Standard (NASB) © 1960, 1962, 1963, 1968, 1971, 1972, 1973, 1975, 1977 by The Lockman Foundation. Used by permission.

> The Holy Bible, New International Version (NIV). Copyright © 1973, 1978, 1984 International Bible Society. Used by permission of Zondervan Publishers.

> The Living Bible (TLB), copyright 1971 by Tyndale House Publishers, Wheaton, Illinois.

Letters and conversations from the DAWSON McALLISTER LIVE! radio show that are included in this volume have been edited and names have been changed to protect the identity of the writers and callers.

Library of Congress Cataloging-in-Publication Data

McAllister, Dawson.
    How to know if you're really in love / Dawson McAllister.
      p. cm.
    ISBN 0–8499–3312–9
    1. Teenagers—Conduct of life—Juvenile literature. 2. Dating (Social customs)—Religious aspects—Christianity—Juvenile literature. 3. Teenagers—Sexual behavior——Juvenile literature. 4. Sexual ethics for teenagers—Juvenile literature. [1. Dating (Social customs) 2. Christian life. 3. Sexual ethics.] I. Title.
HQ35.M393 1994
306.7'0835—dc20
                                   93—40906
                                      CIP
                                      AC

456789 LB 7654321

Printed in the United States of America

Contents

I want to say a very special thank you to
Todd Still, Anthony Kimbrough, and Tim Altman.
They each played a huge part in
the creation of this book.

1

"I Want to Be Loved"

*H*EY, WE'RE NOT JUST TALKING ABOUT A DATE to the prom. We're talking about high stakes. We're talking about *love.*

I know love is high stakes for today's teenagers because you've told me it is. Look at this letter:

Dear Dawson,

Oh, how I long to be loved. To be loved— that's all I want! Really, nothing else matters. Everything else could be taken away from me and I wouldn't care. If only someone would love me.

I've heard it many times and read in the Bible that Jesus loves me, but it doesn't seem to mean anything to me! What's wrong?

I felt you might understand. I don't understand myself. Why do I feel this way? Please, can you help me?

I want to be loved!

This girl is not alone. Students everywhere are saying "I want to be loved." Each week I get letter after letter from teenagers all across this country who want to talk about L-O-V-E. And that's what we're going to do in this book.

4

What Is Love?

Most students want to start by learning what real love is. Yet our society makes that almost impossible.

You are being overwhelmed each day with false information about love and sex. You see adults walk away from their marriages and their families. You see painful mistakes made in relationships every day.

Through advertising and entertainment you can learn all about so-called "safe sex" but virtually nothing about true caring and commitment. And you hear talk about responsibility, about how you should use condoms to practice safe sex. It all reminds me of an old rock song titled "What's Love Got to Do with It?"

No wonder teenagers are confused. No wonder so many of you struggle with how to show love and how to be loved.

OK, so let's start at the beginning and sort it all out. Let's look at the word *love*. That may be where a lot of the confusion starts because we use this word in so many different ways. For example, think about all the things we say we love:

"I love baseball."
"I love apple pie."
"I love Mother."
"I love our dog."
"I love God."
"I love our cabin at the lake."
"I love the flag."
"I love my friends."
"I love my boyfriend (or girlfriend)."

We often use the word *love* when we really mean *like, prefer, enjoy,* or just *had a good time with.* Yes, the path to real love is cluttered with all kinds of confusing words and emotions that may sound like love and feel like love. They may even make us think we are in love. But words and emotions are not the tests of true love, as we'll see as this book unfolds.

Lots of other things cause confusion about love. Day after day I get mail from students who are really struggling with this. Here's a letter from a girl we'll call Sandy:

This is the sob story of two guys and a confused girl. My name is Sandy and I'm 18 years old. Before I go any further let me be sure to tell you that I am a Christian.

There is a guy. His name is Ricky. We have been going together on and off for two years. He loves me a lot and someday wants us to get married. He is a Christian, but he is not helping me in my walk with God. Since we've been going together I have really changed. The worst thing I have done is have sex with him. I know it's wrong, and I knew it was going to be a big mistake, which it was. The main problem is that it took me 16½ years to find a guy who really loves me, and I'm afraid if I let him go it will be a long time before I find someone who loves me that strongly again.

Then there is Robbie. I met him only two weeks ago. I was on a mission trip with my church, and one of my friends went too. She has a brother who goes to college. He came down for two days to visit her. Well, one night I was praying for God to send me a good, Christian guy and the next thing I knew I was hitting it off great with my friend's brother. He went back to college and wrote me a letter asking me out. Even though I'm going with Ricky, I accepted.

Well, I'm not sure if Robbie is going to want to be just friends or want a relationship. Since he is 300 miles away I don't think he's going to want much of a relationship. Ricky loves me, and I love him, but my feelings have not been so strong since I met Robbie. I am starting to think that Robbie may be the one for me. What should I do?

The Emotional Whip-Around

We don't need much more proof than Sandy's letter to see just how confused we can become about love. I call this kind of misery the emotional whip-around. Here's how it works: First we get all tripped up over our needs, emotional needs as well as physical needs. Then someone comes along and seems to fill those needs, and that makes us feel better. The next thing we know, we're telling ourselves we are in love. It doesn't make sense, but it feels good so we buy into it. And then we discover we're wrong. We find out that no one else—no other human being, that is—can really fill our needs. And that hurts.

I recently read a story about a "love network" of men and women who were hoping to meet someone special by sending messages by computer. One lady who was thirty-eight years old had been communicating regularly with a male computer friend. She said he made her feel unique and special. But then she went on to say, "When someone tells you what you need to hear, you begin to wonder if some kind of magic has happened."

Get outta here! This woman thought she had fallen in love with a bunch of computer messages! She thinks some words on a screen can meet all her needs. Here's a thirty-eight-year-old woman who has become irrational about her feelings. Now try and convince me our society hasn't made love a totally confusing concept.

OK, so people make mistakes about love every day. So what's the big deal? That's just part of life.

The big deal is that every day people who are confused about love are getting hurt—really messed up. This isn't some preacher talk. This isn't some theological, seminary kind of deal. Every day, in their search for love, thousands and thousands of people—many of them teenagers—are losing their virginity, getting pregnant, and having abortions. And it doesn't stop there. These "mistakes" in the name of love can eventually lead to more pain and guilt than most of us can imagine.

The Bottom Line

Too many students are desperately looking for real love but finding only cheap and destructive imitations. Too many students think love is a feeling that can come and go quickly. Too many students don't understand that God created love. So our best chance to find real love is to learn from God how He created it to work. If we don't learn from God, then we'll wind up getting bad information.

For example, you may think that being physically attracted to someone is love. You say "Wow, what a hunk!" or "Did you see her?" and you're sure this is it.

But that's not love; that's hormones.

You may think that having someone listen to you and understand you is love. But that's not love; it's kindness.

8

You may think that feeling good when you're around someone is love. That's not love, either; it's attention.

And you may think that having sex is love, but it's not. It's just two amateurs setting off dangerous fireworks.

These are just some of the many ways people confuse real love with something else. The bottom line is this: When you don't understand real love, the way God intended it to be, you can become confused and get hurt, and you can suffer truly painful consequences. Like I said, the stakes are high.

I watched a baseball game once when a pitcher whipped a fastball right by the batter's head. The batter hit the dirt, but got up laughing. Why was he laughing? Because this was an All-Star game. It didn't count in the standings so it really didn't matter to the players. The pitcher threw three more fastballs and the batter, scared from the first wild pitch, never even came close to hitting one. He struck out, big-time, but he walked away laughing along with the pitcher.

Yes, during an All-Star game it was a funny moment, but if they had been facing each other in a World Series, there would have been nothing funny about it. It would have been serious business. The stakes would have been way too high to laugh at.

That's the way it is with this thing called love. It's not a fun game to lose. And yet we all want to play. We all want to be loved. We all find ourselves crying out, as Sandy did, "Please, can you help me? I want to be loved!"

2

Real Love: The Pieces of a Puzzle

SO LOVE IS CONFUSING, AND THE STAKES ARE high. And yes, making wrong choices about love can be painful and even destructive. But here's the encouraging part, the really exciting part: God doesn't want us to be confused about love. He will always point us in the right direction if we will let Him. Remember—and never forget—that God is the author of love.

Dealing with our own sexual desires and learning to relate to the opposite sex is one of the most important issues in life. God understands that, and He wants us to relate to the opposite sex in an exciting and healthy way.

But here's where we usually mess up: We misunderstand what God says about His kind of love, so we usually interpret it in a much too shallow way.

And yet God's way of loving is the key to a meaningful life. It is so important that He wants us to demonstrate it in the way we treat everyone around us.

That includes the people you date.

Wired for Relationships

When it comes to this crazy thing called love, I can't think of anything more encouraging than to know God truly understands. He created us, right? There's nothing

12

He doesn't know about us. He knows the greatest emotional need we have is to love and to be loved. God has wired us for relationships. But those relationships can't fulfill our emotional needs unless we have our priorities straight.

If our priorities follow God's plan, the primary relationship in our lives will be with Him. He, not our boyfriend or girlfriend or anyone else, must be the most important person in our lives. That means the biggest decision in our lives is not who we will marry and love for a lifetime, but whether we will accept the incredible love God offers us through a relationship with Jesus Christ.

I want to share with you now a letter I received from a girl who, through tremendous tragedy, learned about the importance of her love relationship with Jesus Christ:

> Dawson,
>
> I played the Shame Game. My brother molested me when I was four and five years old. My older cousin also began to molest me when our families visited each other. My parents divorced when I was eight. Dad moved overseas for almost seven years. I felt that he left me. I've seen him once a year for ten years.
>
> I went out with lots of guys and I did some pretty risky things—hoping to find the love from a man that would fill the "hole in my soul." But God had His hand on me and by His gentle prodding, I kept my virginity. But I did enough to cut deep wounds. This began in the seventh grade.
>
> I accepted Christ as my Savior near the end of the seventh grade—but that didn't stop me

from throwing myself at the guys and doing the same stuff. I put all the guilt and blame on myself.

Then I met a very special friend. He loved me like no other guy or man has. He gave and gave because he knew I needed love. He never asked for anything but friendship and love in Christ from me. He was my best friend, the closest person to me, next to Christ. Then we broke up after dating a year. We really went through rough times, but I never thought I'd lose him. But even though it hurt I knew it was OK to be away from him because I needed to depend on God, not my boyfriend.

I thought everything was fine—my feelings toward men. I felt I had dealt with the pain, given it to Christ, and left it there. But Satan scratched open that closed wound: Last month, my wonderful stepdad (at least I had thought he was wonderful) came home drunk on my 18th birthday. He never has said, "Happy 18th birthday."

That forced me to remember that humans will fail me. God is the only one I can really trust. He will never leave!

The pain sometimes is still there—memories and thoughts of the past. But God is my best friend and He loves me. Sometimes it's just hard to believe that.

Thank you for discussing this topic on your radio show. This is helping me to continue to give up my pain. I hope every girl will realize love doesn't come in giving your body away. And fathers and brothers may not love you either. But God is the Father who does love you and Jesus is the brother who loves you. Christ will never leave. He's the only one to give your trust to.

14

What a sad, sad story. Here's a girl who has been used and abused, and some of it happened in the name of love. But she knows that wasn't God's love, not even close to it; it wasn't even in the ballpark. She's been through some rough times, but she's learned from them and she's put her trust in God. And that trust lights up all the shadows that otherwise would give her no hope for a happy future.

A Lot to Live Up To

The apostle Paul talks about God's love in 1 Corinthians 13, which many people call the Love Chapter. Let's look at a few of its verses that teach us what love should do and what it shouldn't do.

> **Love is patient, love is kind. It does not envy, it does not boast, it is not proud. It is not rude, it is not self-seeking, it is not easily angered, it keeps no record of wrongs. Love does not delight in evil but rejoices with the truth. It always protects, always trusts, always hopes, always perseveres. Love never fails.**
>
> **1 Cor. 13:4–8** NIV

That's a lot to live up to. God knows how difficult it is. He never said it would be easy. But this is His standard to try for. It can be a mirror we look into to see how our relationships shape up.

It can help answer the question this book is all about: How can you know if you are really in love?

Clearly God has given us guidelines and principles to help us have good, enjoyable relationships with those of the opposite sex. Are you willing to take a really honest look at those principles and hold them up against your relationship with your current boyfriend or girlfriend and your future relationships?

In dating relationships this means choosing to treat the other person with respect and consideration. It means choosing to do what is best for the other person. And it means never intentionally doing anything to hurt the other person, now or in the future. You see, love is more than a feeling or an emotional need. *Love is an act of the will based on respect for and understanding of the other person.*

I hope you're willing to apply God's standards this way because if you are, you'll be on your way to discovering real love in your life.

But first I want you to understand something. Knowing you're really in love is kind of like putting together a puzzle. That's how I want you to look at the rest of this book. In each of the remaining chapters I want to discuss one piece of the love puzzle. We'll use that puzzle piece to apply God's principles and help you complete this statement: "I will know I am developing God's kind of loving relationship when . . ."

You need to remember that each issue we discuss is just one piece of the puzzle. Just because you score OK in one chapter doesn't mean you are really in God's kind of a loving relationship. You must look at the full puzzle.

And finally, keep this very important fact in mind: A love puzzle is never complete without Jesus Christ at its very center. You can bet on it. When you give your date life, your sex life, and your love life to God, He will take control and use these important areas of your life to make you more and more like Jesus. And no one knows more about love. After all, Jesus lived a life of love all the way to the cross:

16

This is my command: Love each other as I have loved you. The greatest love a person can show is to die for his friends.

John 15:12–13

3

Trusting God with Your Love Life

*I will know I am developing
God's kind of loving
relationship when . . .
I turn my date life and
future marriage plans
completely over to God.*

*T*HERE'S NOWHERE ELSE WE CAN BEGIN TALKING about your date life and your love life—except with God Himself. This is so very basic, and yet it's where so many of us mess up every day.

Why do we mess up? Partly because of our emotions, some of the most powerful forces in our lives. Our feelings are real, not just a figment of our imagination, and they play a major role in shaping our lives. God has given us our emotional makeup because He loves us and wants us to enjoy our feelings. But those feelings can be deceptive, eventually making us the fools.

That's why God wants us to be careful. He knows we cannot trust our feelings. Instead we must decide to follow Christ and be led by the Holy Spirit. That means we must obey the truths in the Bible regardless of how we *feel*. In Proverbs 4:23 we read: **"Be careful what you think, because your thoughts run your life."**

God's Number-One Goal

That's easier said than done! Only with God's help can we guard our thoughts. So God's number-one goal for you in all your dating relationships is that you give Him complete control. He wants you to turn over your

20

entire date life and future marriage plans to Him. Think about these questions as you consider your date life:

- Is God in control of your dating relationship?
- If He is, how do you know He is in charge?
- If God is not in control of your date life, how would it change things if He were?

It is easy to allow your dating experiences and dreams of marriage to dominate your life. But when this happens, there is little if any room in your life for God and His guidance. What teenagers often misunderstand is that it is absolutely impossible to have a successful dating relationship and/or marriage unless Jesus Christ is in the driver's seat.

Please don't forget this: When you go after a relationship with the opposite sex more than you go after a relationship with Jesus Christ, conflict will happen. I can promise you that.

Do not be deceived in this area. Your primary goal in life should not be to have a good date life. Instead it should be to love God with all your heart. Someone once said, "God has created us for Himself, and our hearts are restless until we find rest in Him." The reason we were created is to love, worship, and enjoy God.

He doesn't simply want to be a part of your life— He wants to *be* your life. Only when you trust Christ and His ways in everything you do can you have a proper perspective. Remember what Jesus said:

The thing you should want most is God's kingdom and doing what God wants. Then

all these other things you need will be given
to you.

Matt. 6:33

Filling the Hole in Your Heart

God has created us with deep emotional and spiritual needs. Unfortunately, the human tendency is to try and fill these needs with things or with other people, such as a boyfriend or girlfriend. But the people you date can never meet your deepest needs. The Lord is the only One who can fill this hole in your heart.

I received a letter recently from a guy who was trying to meet his needs with his girlfriend rather than with God. Fortunately, his girlfriend was a wise Christian. She was helping him learn the lesson that only God can be God. We can't do His job for Him. Listen to what Ron said:

> It's two o'clock in the morning and I just got off the phone with my girlfriend. She's the one who helped me accept the Lord into my heart.
>
> She shocked me by saying that I should stop idolizing her. After we said good-bye, I realized that in a way I was doing that.
>
> She made me realize that I first have to think about my relationship with God instead of my relationship with her.

Ron learned what we all must learn: While the person you are dating may be terrific, he or she is a sorry God. Humans were never intended to take the place of God in your life.

22

You should never depend on another person to do for you what only Jesus Christ can do. Your dating partner may be wonderful, but he or she can never give you spiritual life. That life comes only from a personal relationship with Jesus Christ.

The Bible tells us:

> **Jesus is the only One who can save people. His name is the only power in the world that has been given to save people. And we must be saved through him.**
>
> **Acts 4:12**

So Jesus is all you need. "No problem," you say. "I can handle that." And then, like the trapeze artist about to leap off the platform and trust that her partner will swing up to catch her, you hesitate. "Are you sure?" you ask. "Are you absolutely, positively sure?"

Hey, no one ever said this trust thing would be a piece of cake. It's easy to slip into a state of panic when you start believing that God is not going to give you the right dating or marriage partner. Some teenagers really worry that God may totally overlook them.

You will never be able to get totally rid of those fears until you can honestly pray this prayer: *God, I place my total trust in You, and I am willing, if You so desire, to go without the privilege of dating or marriage for the rest of my life.*

Whew! That's tough. But we have to do it. We have to believe what the Bible tells us in Romans 8:28:

> **And we know that in all things God works for the good of those who love him, who have been called according to his purpose** (NIV).

So remember—God is on your side. He wants you to be happy, to be content. And if He wants you to have a date life, which He probably does, then He certainly wants you to enjoy it. One of my favorite Bible verses is Jeremiah 29:11; I think it's one of the most encouraging verses in the whole Bible. In it, God gives us this good news:

"I know what I am planning for you," says the LORD, "I have good plans for you, not plans to hurt you. I will give you hope and a good future."

That's exciting! God has plans for you, and that includes your date life. And those plans will work perfectly when you let the Planner control all of your life, including your love life.

A Messed-Up Picture of Reality

But even though we know we should, we don't always give God control.

One of the biggest reasons is PRIDE. Pride is an attitude that places too much importance on self. It makes us feel as if we're better than others. It makes us feel arrogant toward God, as if we don't need Him. And pride keeps us from loving the way God wants us to love.

God hates pride. Proverbs 16:18–19 says:

Pride goes before destruction, a haughty spirit before a fall. Better to be lowly in spirit and among the oppressed than to share plunder with the proud (NIV).

24

Perhaps the greatest problem that pride creates is a messed-up picture of reality. People who have too much pride tend to think the world revolves around them. They believe the world and everyone in it owes them something. They begin to think they are far more important than they really are.

When we act that way around our friends, we're called stuck up and arrogant. But to act that way toward God is just plain foolish.

Prideful people don't understand how dependent they are upon God. They have forgotten that everything they are and everything they have is a gift from God. Apart from God we have absolutely nothing—we *are* nothing.

Service, Sacrifice, and Love

As we ended chapter 2, I mentioned how Jesus is the perfect role model for true love. When He lived on the earth, He was always humble. He was never arrogant. In fact, Jesus left heaven—and remember that's the place with golden streets, fancy mansions, and God Himself—to come to earth and die on the cross for us sinners. As Christians we are to model Jesus' example of service, sacrifice, and love, even in our date lives.

Read Philippians 2:5–8:

In your lives you must think and act like Christ Jesus. Christ himself was like God in everything. But he did not think that being equal with God was something to be used for his own benefit. But he gave up his place with God and made himself nothing. He was

**born to be a man and became like a servant.
And when he was living as a man, he
humbled himself and was fully obedient to
God, even when that caused his death—death
on a cross.**

When Christ was crucified, He was put to the real
test, the biggest of all finals. On that cross the love of
Christ and His compassion went head to head with the
sickness of sin and hatred. But even then, Jesus contin-
ued to love us humbly and willingly.

We should follow His example. We must focus on
Him and not on others, including boyfriends or girlfriends.
That's what the Bible tells us to do in Hebrews 12:2:

**Let us look only to Jesus, the One who
began our faith and who makes it perfect. He
suffered death on the cross. But he accepted
the shame as if it were nothing because of the
joy that God put before him. And now he is
sitting at the right side of God's throne.**

Facing Difficult Times

None of you will ever suffer as Jesus did on that
cross. But you will have difficult times and difficult
relationships, especially as you begin to date. These
difficult times will test your ability to love in God's way.

It won't be easy. It's something you'll have to work
at your entire life. We all must work on this. To succeed,
we must depend on God to help us have His kind of
love. He has to be the centerpiece of our lives, including
dating relationships. And one piece of the love puzzle

26

that cannot be left out is the decision to trust God completely with your love life.

Have you done it?

4

Dating in the Will of God

I will know I am developing God's kind of loving relationship when . . . I am dating someone within God's will.

THIS DATING GUIDELINE SHOULD BE A NO-BRAINER, as simple as 2 + 2 = 4. Simply put, if you are a Christian, God does not want you to date someone who is not a Christian.

But don't just take my word for it. Take God's Word in 2 Corinthians 6:14–15:

> **You are not the same as those who do not believe. So do not join yourselves to them. Good and bad do not belong together. Light and darkness cannot share together. How can Christ and Belial, the devil, have any agreement? What can a believer have together with a nonbeliever?**

You may already have formed your opinion about whether you should date non-Christians. Maybe you think it's OK. Maybe you say, "Oh, we're not really serious. We just enjoy spending time together. We won't ever fall in love."

Don't give me that line. It won't cut it, and God won't buy it.

A Tough Piece of the Love Puzzle

Because He loves us so much, God wants us to focus our attention and energy on loving Him. (We talked about this in the previous chapters.) So it should be clear that God wants our date life to help us focus on Him, rather than turning our attention to something or someone else. God is completely wise; He knows a non-Christian will not help us keep our attention on Him.

But I know this guideline about Christians dating non-Christians is something teenagers struggle with each day. It's a tough piece of the love puzzle.

How do I know? Because I talk to students and get letters and questions about this principle all the time. I have a live call-in radio talk show for students called DAWSON McALLISTER LIVE! The topic of one of my recent shows was the same as this book—How can you know whether you are really in love? And guess what the show's very first call was about? You guessed it. A Christian girl called in to ask about dating a guy who wasn't a Christian.

When I asked this girl (let's call her Megan) why she thought she might be in love, she answered, "Because I feel comfortable around him. I just do."

"Is he a Christian?" I asked.

"No, he's a Buddhist," she said.

"*Whoa!* Stop right there!" I didn't need to know anything else about this guy, whoever he was. I had all the information I needed to give Megan her answer. What follows is my response to her:

> I don't want to get in a big argument or
> debate with you, but it's not God's will that

you date him or marry him. So whatever emotion you have, Megan, that emotion is not from God.

The only One who can really give us God's counsel on love is God, Himself, because God *is* love. And He says don't be teamed up with those who aren't Christians; those are true statements from God's Word, God's counsel.

One of the biggest tests of our Christian lives, and I think it's probably one of the biggest tests of your life right now, is whether you're going to listen to God's counsel about love and who to date and who not to date—or whether you will simply follow your emotions.

You can't say, "I know it will be God's will that I date someone or marry someone when I know he's not a Christian." Because that's not really love. That may be your emotions, all stirred up, but it's not love.

Megan then told me about a friend (some friend this must have been!) who encouraged her to give up her Christian faith and become a Buddhist like her boyfriend.

"No guy's worth that!" I told her. "I think it's out of God's will that you date this guy, flat out," I said. "If you date him at all, you're out of God's will. As we used to say, I wouldn't warm my hands at that fire very long. . . .

So my prediction for you, Megan, is that the biggest decision you will make that will affect your relationship with God more than anything

else in your high school and even college years
is what you do with this guy.

It's a big decision, isn't it? But it's easy to
know which way to decide because God says
break up. This is where it all hits the fan—how
much do you love God?

I don't know whether Megan followed God's advice and broke up with her boyfriend. I don't know
whether she's now placing her focus on her relationship
with Jesus Christ. But I do know this: The lifestyle of a
non-Christian is radically different than the lifestyle of a
Christian (that is, if the Christian is living as God wants
him or her to live).

Conflicting Views of Love

None of this means I am condemning non-Christians.
What it does mean is that a Christian's idea of love and a
non-Christian's idea of love are two completely different
things. The Christian's idea is based on the Bible, which
says real love comes from God because God is love.

Look at 1 John 4:7–8:

**Dear friends, we should love each other,
because love comes from God. Everyone who
loves has become God's child and knows
God. Whoever does not love does not know
God, because God is love.**

A non-Christian does not have a personal relationship with Jesus Christ, so how can that person love you
with God's kind of love? If someone doesn't know God,

he or she doesn't have God's love. And without God's love, that person doesn't have the power to love you as God wants him or her to love you. Together, the two of you cannot—absolutely cannot—be in God's kind of a loving relationship.

Let's go a step further and look at what God tells us about non-Christians and where they place their focus.

> **In the past we were foolish. We did not obey, we were wrong, and we were slaves to many things our bodies wanted and enjoyed. We spent our lives doing evil and being jealous. People hated us, and we hated each other.**
>
> **Titus 3:3**

This verse describes the heart and mind of non-Christians. It calls them foolish. It calls them disobedient. It says they are slaves to all kinds of bodily pleasures. (This includes things like sexual kicks and anything else that pushes God away.) Finally, it says they have a lifestyle of evil, jealousy, and hate. In other words, they are never happy with what they have, and they're convinced that everyone else has something they deserve. Not a pretty picture of someone you might spend the rest of your life with!

Incredibly, even with such clear warnings from God's Word, too many teenagers—like Megan—still want to experiment. They still want to test God's Word and take a chance on dating a non-Christian. They don't seem to understand that when they spend a lot of time with someone an emotional partnership is formed. It's a strong bond. And it almost always leads to a strong desire to please that person by accepting and even imitating his or her actions, thoughts, and responses.

Non-Christians' values on dating, sex, and life in general are not based on biblical truth. And non-Christians don't have the power of Christ to help them exercise self-control. That means non-Christian dating partners are more likely to lead you into difficult (as if any are easy) sexual temptations.

Now I know some of you are telling yourselves you are just doing some "missionary dating." (That's where Christians date non-Christians thinking they can help lead them to Christ.) Hang it up. Forget it. Don't you think God is big enough, powerful enough, and loving enough to find another way to draw that person to Himself? I guarantee you He is. I also guarantee you that He never contradicts Himself—God will never ask you to violate His word, such as by dating a non-Christian, so that something good can happen. In most cases of missionary dating, the Christian ends up abandoning his or her commitment to Christ to keep from losing the relationship. It just doesn't work.

I got a letter from a girl who had tried it. She was a strong Christian and had started dating a non-Christian guy. She thought she could get him to come to church with her and eventually become a Christian. It never happened.

What happened, instead, was that she became more and more attracted to him, not only physically, but emotionally. She was forming that emotional partnership I told you about. She was bonding. She began to believe he was meeting a need in her life that hadn't been met before. But deep down inside, this girl knew she shouldn't get involved with this guy. She knew what God's Word said.

She had a decision to make, the same decision Megan had to make. She had to decide whether to obey God and break up with her boyfriend or ignore God and keep getting more and more involved with her "new love." She didn't break up. Instead, she wrote to me hoping I would tell her everything would work out. If she wanted an excuse, she wrote to the wrong person! I told her she was choosing her boyfriend over God. I told her she was making a bad decision. I wish I knew what happened, but I don't. I never heard from her again.

When you push aside God's advice and date a non-Christian, you are saying that God cannot meet your need for love and acceptance. So you decide to "play God."

There was a song in the eighties that included the words, "How can it be wrong when it feels so right?" Now those are dangerous words! They take us back to believing in our feelings even when the Bible tells us to do otherwise. And when we give in to our feelings, we give up self-control. But here's the worst part: Non-Christians have needs, too, but they can't turn to God to have those needs met. And they can't turn to God for the self-control they need to say no to sex. So when a Christian dates a non-Christian, the result is two people spending lots of time with each other and neither having self-control. That's a formula for disaster.

Don't Play Games with God

So don't try and play games with this piece of the love puzzle. Don't try to play games with God. A dating relationship between a Christian and a non-Christian is not based on real love. It can't be.

You have to come to the place where you believe God loves you and will meet your deepest needs. You have to believe Him, completely and totally. You must let Him be God. Quit trying to be your own god. Wait on Him to give you what's best for you at the right time.

Remember, if you are a Christian, you should obey God's counsel. In the case of dating non-Christians, His counsel is clear and it shouldn't be mocked. Jesus said,

> **Why do you call me, "Lord, Lord," but do not do what I say?**
> **Luke 6:46**

Are you doing what God says in this area of your dating life? If not, I want to let another student give you some encouragement. Here's a letter written to me by a girl we'll call Linda who struggled with dating a non-Christian and then, with God's help, did the right thing.

Dear Dawson,

I went to your conference on dating and teens. And now, I've finally broken up with my boyfriend. It was the hardest thing I've ever done in my life.

I did it this morning after months of turning my back on God. I've grown up in a strong Christian home and have been a Christian for eight years. I fell in love with a good-looking non-Christian guy who has a wonderful personality.

For six months I let him and Satan control my life. I knew all along our relationship was sinful but I kept denying it. I've learned so much throughout the last six months about what God will do to your life if you turn your back on Him.

Slowly I learned that the relationship I was in was wrong, and finally after many months of him talking me into doing things with him we almost had sex. I said no and walked away, but he kept saying how premarital sex is OK. A couple of times he had me convinced. But finally, I broke off our relationship for good!!!

Your conference really helped me after months of stubbornness. Now God is back in control of my life for good. Your words of wisdom through-out the conference kept playing in my mind over and over. Never again will I let young, innocent love control my life. God taught me a lesson and He sure did teach it well.

When I broke up with my boyfriend, I explained how it was what God wanted me to do. With him being a non-Christian, he didn't understand at all.

I now know to never run from God. It just gets you into worse trouble!

5

Making the Right Choices

*I will know I am developing
God's kind of loving
relationship when . . .
I am only dating Christians
who are growing spiritually.*

*I*N THE LAST CHAPTER WE TALKED ABOUT HOW IMPORTANT IT IS to date Christians only and to avoid a dating relationship with an unbeliever. Now here's another piece of our love puzzle that fits right next to that one: Christians should only be dating other Christians who are trying to follow God on a daily basis, who are completely focused on growing to be more and more like Jesus Christ.

The question is, how do we tell the difference between a Christian who is growing in faith and someone who may be a Christian in name only? Here's a guideline: Some people say they are Christians but don't act like Christians. Therefore, watch a potential dating partner's actions before you go out with him or her.

God wants you to avoid dating Christians who repeatedly disobey Him as part of their lifestyle. The reason is clear: There is almost no difference between dating a non-Christian and dating a Christian who is not walking with God. Several of the problems with dating a non-Christian that were discussed in the previous chapter also occur when you date a "name-only" Christian.

A Dangerous Situation

People who claim to be Christians, yet live a life of disobedience to God aren't likely to obey God's commands regarding sexuality. Also, because they aren't walking with God, they may have little self-control. You put those two things together—disobeying God's commands and no self-control—and you've got a dangerous sexual situation when it comes to dating.

One of the most important things the Bible encourages us to do is spend time with other Christians. God knows that dating other Christians—Christians walking close to Him—can help you overcome sexual temptation.

In 2 Timothy 2:22, God reminds us about the kind of people we should spend time with:

> **Run away from the evil young people like to do. Try hard to live right and to have faith, love, and peace, together with those who trust in the Lord from pure hearts.**

Christ wants you to spend most of your time with people who really want to know God. Because their standards are similar to yours, you are more likely to help one another stay away from lust.

Remember King David? He had weaknesses, but he also had a strength you should look for in the people you date. He decided that seeking God was the highest priority in his life. He talked about that priority in Psalm 27:4:

> **The one thing I want from God, the thing I seek most of all, is the privilege of meditating in his temple, living in his presence every**

day of my life, delighting in his incomparable perfections and glory. (TLB)

Christians with that kind of an attitude are the dating partners God wants you to have. The problem is, lots of people who claim to be Christians are not living like Christians. They may show up in church to hear what God's Word says, but they don't take the message with them when they leave. As you think about a dating partner, see if he or she measures up to the challenge found in James 1:22:

Do what God's teaching says; when you only listen and do nothing you are fooling yourselves.

Does your dating partner just claiming to be a Christian, or does he or she do what the Bible says to do?

Any Christian who is trying to obey God on a daily basis will have Christ as the foundation of his or her life. Dating relationships are no different. A dating relationship that honors God and has His approval will have Christ at the center. Relationships built on anything other than Christ are shaky and suspect.

What about You?

But let's stop and change gears. So far this chapter has focused on the spiritual condition of your potential dating partner. Now I want you to think about yourself for a moment. No matter how strong you are spiritually, you know how difficult it is to live like God wants you

44

to live. There are going to be times when you will face severe temptations, and sometimes you are going to fail.

A strong Christian dating partner can help you get back on track and help protect you from your own weaknesses. Look at what the Bible says about two people who are working toward the same goal:

> **Two people are better than one because they get more done by working together. If one falls down, the other can help him up.**
>
> **Eccles. 4:9–10a**

God is honored when both dating partners are helping each other grow closer to Him. In contrast, there is nothing good about a strong Christian being pulled into sin by a partner who isn't really serious about God.

In the last chapter we talked about how foolish, disobedient, and envious non-Christians are. We talked about how they focus on all the wrong things. Let's now look at what the Bible tells us *we* should be focusing our thoughts upon:

> **Brothers and sisters, think about the things that are good and worthy of praise. Think about the things that are true and honorable and right and pure and beautiful and respected.**
>
> **Phil. 4:8**

One of the best ways to make good choices about who you will date is to be sure your thought life passes the Philippians 4:8 test. Let's look at some of the words this verse uses to describe a godly thought life and consider how those words relate to your thinking about dating.

Good thinking means focusing your attention on what is constructive and healthy.

True thinking means comparing everything you see with the way God says things really are.

Right thinking means making up your mind to do what is right no matter what the cost.

Pure thinking means caring about the other person's reputation even more than your own.

Adopting Philippians 4:8 thinking is evidence that Christ is in control of your life. It is also something you should look for in a dating partner.

Remember this: Thoughts quickly turn into actions. If you or your dating partner are not focusing your *thoughts* on what is good, true, honorable, right, and pure, your dating *actions* may soon be ones you'll regret.

Let me summarize this as clearly as I can: Look for dating partners who are strong Christians. And whatever you do, don't compromise your standards just to get a date. It's not worth it.

Is This the Right Person for You?

Following are some questions you can ask yourself about your current or future dating partners. The answers—if you answer them honestly—can help you decide if that person is the kind of person God would want you to date. Don't expect perfection because you'll never find it. But remember that God does expect you to set standards and stick by them.

- Does my dating partner listen to me and respect my point of view?
- Does my dating partner make unreasonable demands on me?
- Is my dating partner kind to me and sensitive to my feelings?
- Does my dating partner influence me to live a sexually pure life?
- How does my dating partner treat his or her parents?
- Is my dating partner actively seeking to know God better?
- Does my dating partner talk to me about spiritual things?
- Does my dating partner talk about how he or she wants me to fit into God's plans?

Here's part of a letter I received from a girl we'll call Laura, a girl who learned how important it is to date a Christian and how it can hurt if you don't:

> About a month ago my boyfriend broke up with me. We're both 16. He said his dad was pressuring him because we were too serious. I agree we were a little serious. We spent too much time alone.
>
> Every day that week I cried two to three hours. I couldn't do my homework. I couldn't concentrate. I was very depressed.
>
> From what I hear he had been wanting to break up with me for a couple of months. He had been spending less and less time with me and

more and more time with his friends. I could see it coming, but I didn't think it would be this bad.

He is a Christian, but he's not a very strong Christian. I am, but he did come between me and the Lord.

Looking back, breaking up was good because we would have both been hurt more if it happened later. We were physical, though we never had sex and weren't about to. We would have been deeply hurt because of it. At first we were friends. Then it grew into a relationship and a very good one. But after about six months it became physical. That's when it took a dive.

I've been hurt so much by the way he has treated me after we broke up. I don't want to have a boyfriend anymore. I never want to love again.

Right now what I want for his life and mine is that we can become closer to God and have a deep relationship with Him.

Please don't let Laura's story become your story. Find a dating partner who's serious about his or her relationship with God. When you do you'll be one step closer to having God's kind of love.

6

Are You Willing to Wait for Real Love?

I will know I am developing God's kind of loving relationship when . . . I am willing to wait.

I DON'T KNOW ABOUT YOU, BUT I HATE TO WAIT. I don't think anyone likes it. It's hard to wait on anything when just about everything in our lives is "fast" this and "instant" that.

We've got fast food, Minute Rice, and instant coffee. We've got express lines at the bank and the grocery store. We even have call waiting on our phones (which really isn't waiting at all—its whole purpose is to help us avoid waiting by taking every call the moment it comes in).

The problem with living in an instant world is that we can find ourselves wanting instant love as well. We don't want to wait for it. But waiting is one of the ways God protects us from bad choices.

I need you to hear this loud and clear: There's nothing instant about love. And there's nothing more important to a loving relationship than patience.

Back in chapter 2 we looked at some verses from 1 Corinthians 13, the Love Chapter. That passage starts out with a description of what love is. The first characteristic given is patience: "Love is patient." (Keep in mind that the love described in 1 Corinthians 13 has to do with the way all Christians should relate to each other. It includes romantic love, but it is much bigger than that.)

The Rush Trap

Before you are engaged or married (if you're lucky), you and your dating partner will discover some things about each other that are less than perfect. In marriage, patient love means you are choosing to love and be committed to your partner for a lifetime despite his or her "imperfections." Believe me, this is a big deal. No matter how long two people have been married or how much in love they are, both will have to practice a large dose of patient love to keep their marriage healthy.

But patient love also plays a very important part in a dating relationship. From the very first moment you meet a potential dating partner you need to practice patient love. How? By committing yourself to protecting his or her reputation and dignity no matter how much your feelings tempt you to go a little further. If you don't, you may find yourselves caught up in the rush trap.

The rush trap is a giant hole teenagers often dig for themselves as they travel down Romance Road with the opposite sex. Here's how it works: First you allow yourself to become overwhelmed with good feelings and exciting emotions when you're with that person. Everything "feels so right" that you lose your objectivity.

Too many people allow this to happen in crucial decisions that can greatly affect the rest of their lives. Guided by their feelings, they make bad decisions such as sex before marriage, a quick engagement, or a premature marriage. Then, too late, they discover they were not in love at all.

I can't think of anything more painful then watching what someone thought was love turn into disappointment, then hurt, then eventually into deep scars. And all too often that "instant love" produces an innocent child who will bear the pain of the parents' mistakes the rest of his or her life.

How do I know the rush trap is so dangerous? Because you've told me so in your letters and at conferences and on my radio show. In fact, a little while ago, a guy we'll call Chris called in to the show. He had fallen into the rush trap, big-time.

He told me he had just started seeing a girl who had another boyfriend. He had met her at a dance, he said, and they had been seeing each other off and on for about two months. But then she told him she was pregnant by her other boyfriend.

Chris, who was eighteen years old, said her pregnancy didn't bother him too much because he was "very deeply in love with her."

My first comment to Chris was, "You better let this ride for a while." Here's how the rest of the conversation went:

> Chris: Oh, we're not going to get married right away, we're going to try to live together for a while.

> Dawson: Whoa, whoa, whoa . . . hold the phone here! Let's start over. First of all, you don't want to live with her because when you live with her you're disobeying God big-time because you didn't get married and make the commitment to marriage. And secondly . . . emotionally you'll think you're married because

you'll be sleeping with her. And then when you break up it will be just like getting a divorce. The problem is she never got the commitment from you to begin with. It's a lifetime thing. I don't want to rain on your parade, but I don't want to see you make a lot of mistakes, either.

Do you know the Lord, Chris?

Chris: Yes sir.

Dawson: Well, if you really know Christ, you know God just doesn't get off on having people live together who aren't married.

Chris: Yeah, but we're going to do the engagement thing.

Dawson: Yeah, but you still don't live together when you're engaged. What you need, the best friend you've got, is time. . . . This girl's emotions are whipped every which way but loose. I mean, her glands are on the ceiling somewhere with this baby. She doesn't even know what she thinks. She's got this other guy who's gotten her pregnant and she doesn't know what she thinks about him. She gave it all away for him. And now we've got you coming in and she's confused about you. This girl needs to settle down. And you need to settle down,

too, and give it time—and more time.
Don't let your glands think it's love,
and don't let someone else's emotional
needs and your meeting them think
that's love. Give it some time.

Whew! Chris is in for a lot of trouble if he doesn't slow down. He needs time to think objectively about his dating partner. Right now he's letting his emotions make the big decisions. Instead he ought to step back from this situation and seek God's plans for him.

Love Versus Infatuation

Let's think about the bigger picture for a moment. Because God loves us, He has given us some guidelines in His word to help us understand the difference between genuine love and what appears to be love (infatuation).

Infatuation is the impulsive, emotional side of love. It is based on a partial knowledge of the other person, but it is not true love because it has not faced the tests of time and difficult circumstances. Though infatuation is not true love, it often passes for it. Think of all the advertisements, television shows, movies, and popular songs that suggest love is nothing more than infatuation.

Don't misunderstand; we have all been there. It is common to become infatuated at the beginning of a new relationship, and there is nothing wrong with that. You can't eat, you can't sleep, and you can't stop thinking about that person. However, no matter how incredibly, painfully wonderful it may feel, it is not a smart idea to

56

allow yourself to be controlled by infatuation.

In the eyes of the world, love is an intense *feeling* that overcomes two people who are "right for each other." Do you see the problem with this? With infatuation feelings are the controlling factor; the foundation of the relationship becomes how the two people *feel* about each other. Then when their feelings change (and trust me, they will) they aren't in love anymore. So they have to try and find a way to get "that lovin' feeling" back. Maybe they'll try more kissing, more touching, or even going all the way. And if they can't, the relationship ends, often with deep pain and regrets.

Infatuation says love is blind. But that's crazy. Love is *not* blind. The person who blindly denies the faults of another person is caught up in infatuation. Remember, God's kind of love isn't blind. If it was, Jesus Christ would never have had to die on the cross for our sins—because God would not have seen our sins.

Real, genuine love—God's kind of love—looks realistically at the weaknesses of another person. It deals with that person in a non-judging, accepting way. God's kind of love evaluates the other person *carefully*. Although this kind of true love can begin with infatuation, it never stays there.

In contrast, uncontrolled infatuation will rush a relationship to romance so that the intense feelings may be kept alive. When you're infatuated with someone you're in a big hurry for many things, such as:

Security—assurance that the other person will not leave you.

Acceptance—being loved just as you are.

Affection—an aroused feeling of intimacy, usually due to some form of sexual activity.

Adventure—a desire to seek and enjoy new experiences together, so the old doesn't wear off.

All of these things are by-products of healthy, God's-kind-of-love relationships, but they're rare when a relationship is based on infatuation. To some degree these characteristics can be found in dating relationships, but they should be carefully saved and guarded until the commitment of marriage frees you to explore them more fully together.

Uncontrolled infatuation is selfish. It is always more interested in what the relationship produces (what will I get?) than in showing real love (what can I give?). Infatuated people will say and do almost anything to keep those addictive, intense, romantic feelings alive. That's like picking the blooms off a fruit tree. They look good, they smell good; but the moment you pick them, they die. Worst of all, the tree will never produce real fruit without those blooms. And that's exactly what happens to a relationship controlled by infatuation rather than godly patience.

Some people will suggest there is such a thing as love at first sight. Forget that. It can't happen. There may be a strong attraction at first sight. You may even sense that "this is the right person for me." But don't try to convince yourself that what you're feeling is love. Love is not something you catch, like the flu. Love is like a garden. It grows slowly and takes a lot of care and nurturing. Real love, genuine love, God's kind of love is going to cost you time, time, and more time. So be patient.

Remember, we are all experts at hiding the parts of ourselves we don't think others will like. That's why discovering the true character of the person you are dating is a process you should never rush. If you feel

58

you may be in love, remind yourself to take it slowly because time is on your side.

Showing Patient Love

Before we close this chapter, let's talk a little bit more about how we can learn to show patient love.

There is no way we can love patiently, the way God wants us to, by ourselves. We have to get help from Him; His love is perfectly patient. Jesus is our model of patience. We are told in 1 Peter to imitate Jesus' example.

> **This is what you were called to do because Christ suffered for you and gave you an example to follow. So you should do as he did. He had never sinned and he had never lied. People insulted Christ, but he did not insult them in return. Christ suffered, but he did not threaten. He let God, the One who judges rightly, take care of him.**
>
> **1 Pet. 2:21–23**

When Jesus hung on the cross for our sins, people hurled horrible insults at Him. He could have come off the cross right then. He had the power to do it. He could have taken matters into his own hands and destroyed them on the spot. But instead, He chose to sacrifice His right to revenge, His dignity, and His very life. His love for God and for us was incredibly, overwhelmingly patient. He committed Himself to following God's plan to save us, no matter what it cost. Why? Because He had complete trust that God would take care of Him.

God has given us that same promise. He will take care of us. And that means He'll take care of our dating relationships too. The only question is whether we'll give Him the time to do it.

Will you be patient? Will you stay away from the rush trap? Will you wait on God? If you do, I promise He will not let you down.

7

Love and Friendship Grow Hand in Hand

I will know I am developing God's kind of loving relationship when . . . the person I am dating is one of my closest friends.

MANY STUDENTS ARE CONVINCED THAT SOME-
WHERE OUT THERE is that one special person. They are stuck in
what I call the "either/or syndrome," which goes like this:
"The reason I am dating is to find that one special person.
I don't have time for a relationship if it doesn't quickly
develop into a steady thing. Either my dating partner
and I feel something special soon, or I'm outta here."

The problem with this attitude is that it causes us to
miss opportunities to form great friendships, friendships that will be there for us long after most of our
romances are distant memories.

The Bible has a lot to say about the importance of
having good friends. Proverbs 17:17 tells us:

**A friend loves you all the time, and a
brother helps in time of trouble.**

The either/or syndrome is a thief that can rob you of
some terrific relationships, friendships that can be more
fulfilling than most people realize. If you aren't willing
to go out on a date just for fun then you may be caught
in the either/or syndrome.

Rather than focusing all of your dating opportunities on finding "the right one," relax a little. God may

have some other opportunities in store for you. He may want to use friendship dates to help you learn things about yourself and the opposite sex that you don't yet know, things that may make you better prepared for when someone special does come along.

If your friendship with a member of the opposite sex grows into a romantic relationship, that's great. Thank God for it. And if it simply grows into deeper friendship, then you still win. I've never heard anyone say, "I've got too many friends who love and accept me for who I am."

Here's the point: Getting caught up in the either/or syndrome is a waste of time. If you give your energy to making new friends feel loved, God may one day surprise you by turning a special friend into a lover.

The Blessings of Friendship

A while back, I did one of my radio shows on spiritual friendships. I invited students to call in and tell about a special friend who had really helped them walk with Christ. One of the callers was a girl we'll call Karen. She was a nineteen-year-old from Tennessee. Here's a portion of what she said:

> We were friends first. It started out as purely a friendship relationship. And then all of a sudden we kind of realized we had stronger feelings for each other.
>
> It didn't dawn on me that I was in love with the guy until I was in Sunday school one day and we were talking about love. We were studying 1 Corinthians 13.

I realized it's a perfect definition of the
love in our relationship. It was just really great.
And he loves me back in the same way.

The best part is that they're planning on getting
married next year.

I always like it when people tell me their relationship started out as a friendship. It means that the more
they learned about one another, the more they loved one
another. Their love is based on really knowing and
accepting each other, not on passion.

Sometimes that's all a dating relationship starts
with, nothing but passion. And that's dangerous. When
two flamethrowers get together, the relationship seldom
survives the heat. And all too often, someone gets
burned.

So hey, I'll take friendship as a starting point any day
of the week. In the end, passion will take care of itself.

God's Ultimate Plan

God has designed life so that all of us need friends.
And He wants us to have healthy friendships with
members of both sexes. But sometimes we get in such a
hurry to find a hot date that we miss a great friendship.
We forget:

- That life isn't easy and we need the support
  of friends.
- That friends help us grow spiritually.
- That friends often encourage us when we
  need it most.

66

God's ultimate goal for every Christian is *not* helping us find someone to date, fall in love with, and marry. His ultimate goal is helping us become more like Christ. Relationships are tools in the hand of God to accomplish our spiritual growth. God gives us opportunities for friendships with both sexes to help us grow in many ways including:

- Learning more about who we are.
- Discovering our strengths and weaknesses.
- Understanding the concepts of kindness and generosity.

We need friendships to be the kind of people God wants us to be. The Bible tells us:

As iron sharpens iron, so people can improve each other.
Prov. 27:17

God has made males and females differently. (Oh really, Dawson! What was your first clue?) Here's the point: Men and women have different ways of looking at many things, and we have a lot we can learn from each. For example, generally speaking, women can help men be more sensitive and creative while men can help women be more rational and secure. If girls spend time with the right kind of guys, and guys with the right kind of girls, then both will grow. Friendship dating is a God-given opportunity for you to do that: to grow emotionally, socially, and spiritually.

Here's something else: All of us have certain needs, and God uses all kinds of ways to help us meet those needs. Dating gives you a chance to become God's partner in meeting the needs of another person.

So here's the big pitch: Never separate friendship from dating. You need to be friends with the people you date, and you need to date people who are your friends. If you do that, your dating relationships will be more godly, more fun, and more successful.

Donna called my radio show a while back to talk about what she thinks is important to a dating relationship.

> My boyfriend and I have been going out for almost four years and the one thing that's really good in our relationship is encouragement. We encourage each other in the Lord and I think that is something that has to be in a love relationship.

She's right. Encouragement grows out of friendship. So don't blow off friendships in a mad rush to find a date for Friday night. When that date is long forgotten, your friends will still be your friends.

8

Telling Each Other the Truth

I will know I am developing God's kind of loving relationship when . . . my dating partner and I can tell each other the truth.

*T*HIS IS THE COMMUNICATION PART OF OUR LOVE
PUZZLE. We're talking about honesty here. We're talking
about sharing whatever thoughts and feelings are neces-
sary to make the relationship more Christlike.

I'm not talking about surface-buzz chitchat here.
It's easy to talk with the guys about sports and cars and
girls and homework. It's easy to talk with the girls about
clothes and cars and guys and homework. But when it
comes to serious talk, stuff below the surface—the
things we keep locked inside that really matter—it's not
always so easy.

Deep, honest communication is seldom easy for
anyone. Think how difficult it can be to talk with your
parents about certain issues. Think how hard it is to talk
to your best friend about how he or she hurt your feelings. Think how tough it can be to talk with your youth
pastor about a spiritual problem you may be having.

When the issues are personal or emotional it can be
even harder. Obviously, most dating relationships are
both personal and emotional. However, that makes
direct, honest communication even more important.

Truth Versus Evil

Let's look at another characteristic of God's kind of love from 1 Corinthians 13. Verse 6 tells us that

Love is not happy with evil, but is happy with the truth.

OK, this is a two-parter. First the positive: The truth makes love happy. *Truth* here does not mean telling someone you don't like the way she wears her hair, or that his shoes are funny, or that he has bad breath. Truth means important things about life and God that will help one or both of you be better Christians.

For example, if the way a girl dresses is causing her boyfriend to struggle with lust, he should ask her to change so that their relationship doesn't get sidetracked by hormones. Or if a guy plans a date with a little "park-in-the-dark-and-let's-see-what-happens" time thrown in, his girlfriend needs to say, "No thanks. I don't think that's what God had in mind for this date."

WARNING: Think before you speak! Especially you guys. Honesty doesn't mean being cold, rude, or arrogant. Make your point, but be as kind and gentle as you can.

All right, now let's look at the second part of this verse. *Evil* makes love unhappy. Since our context is truth, let's change the word *evil* to *untruth*. If we are untruthful with each other, big problems can be created.

What do I mean? It's like this. Men and women react differently to the spoken word. For example, girls tend to believe everything guys tell them, especially when it's a personal compliment or an expression of affection. They are very good at romanticizing what guys say. Words are very important to them.

On the other hand, guys tend to speak using their glands first and their brains second. Guys use words like tools to help them get something they want. That might be good in debate class, but it can do real damage on date night. Here's a sample of what can happen.

The guy will say, "I think you're one of the nicest girls I've met" (meaning *in the last thirty seconds*). It's not untrue, but it is manipulation.

And how does the girl hear this? She believes, *He just said I'm the nicest girl he's ever met. He must mean I'm the only girl he ever wants to meet.*

He carefully shades the truth in the hope that she'll want to participate in a little lip-lock with him. She, on the other hand, thought she heard romance, love, and maybe even marriage knocking on her door.

As funny as this illustration might sound, the Bible looks at this as a kind of evil. It certainly isn't God's kind of love, and in the end it will lead to unhappiness.

God demands that we be honest with each other at all times, and that includes in our dating relationships. Ephesians 4:25 lays it on the line:

> **So you must stop telling lies. Tell each other the truth, because we all belong to each other in the same body** (that is, the body of Christ, the church).

There are no exceptions. God wants us to tell the truth . . . and He doesn't say it's OK to stretch it either! Remember, *God is truth.* And Jesus told us in John 14:6,

> **I am the way, the truth, and the life.**

74

Truth in our dating relationships is a necessity. And I'm not just talking about *telling* the truth. When the Bible says that "love is happy with the truth," it also means that the best thing for every relationship is to hear the truth and to see things as they really are. Love thrives on reality, not fantasy, and certainly not on manipulation.

So how does being "happy with the truth" play out in the dating game? When we are happy with the truth we will look at our relationships more honestly. We will be more realistic and face the facts. We will try to avoid romanticizing the relationship and make it something it really isn't.

Several months ago, a girl in Texas named Sandra called in to DAWSON McALLISTER LIVE! about the incredible openness and honesty between her and her boyfriend. Here's part of that call. I think it's a great illustration of a God-controlled relationship:

Sharon: My boyfriend made me promise him two things after we started seeing each other. Number one is that Christ will always be the center of my life. He made me promise that.

Dawson: How did you feel when he made you promise that?

Sharon: It kind of made me melt.

Dawson: What was the second promise?

Sharon: That no matter what happened, if he ever did anything to make me upset, make me feel uncomfortable or

anything, to tell him. And you know,
that's hard, to tell somebody, "Hey,
you're making me mad" or whatever.
But he made me promise him that too.

Dawson: Have you done that?

Sharon: Pretty much so.

Dawson: Like what?

Sharon: I told him that I thought we were
going too fast, and he understood that.

Now there's a relationship that's "happy in the
truth." Sandra and her boyfriend have learned to honestly talk about things that bother them. All dating
relationships need to have that kind of openness. Over
the long run, it will make you much happier.

Are You Afraid of the Truth?

Unfortunately, many students haven't yet learned
the benefits of relationships based on truth and honesty.
And the result is that they are getting hurt, really hurt.

Here's part of a letter from a girl we'll call April.
Count up how many times April and her boyfriend
were dishonest with themselves and with each other.

> Six months after I had been going out with Kevin,
> I found out I was pregnant. I thought, I'll keep the
> baby and Kevin and I will someday get married be-
> cause I know he really loves me, and would never
> leave me.
> Well, I told him I thought I was pregnant and
> after telling him that I wanted to keep the baby,

he said, "Fine, but I'm not the one who's going to tell your dad."

April's story goes on to say she ended up lying to her parents about the pregnancy and about the abortion she eventually had. She stopped going to church, and soon after the abortion she learned Kevin had been having sex with another girl.

I hurt for this girl. She's in real pain. She lied to her parents. She lied to herself. She probably lied to many of her friends. And who knows how many lies Kevin told?

There wasn't much joy in that relationship, was there? No, and there never will be. There never can be joy in a relationship when truth is left out.

So let's get personal. How can you know if you and your dating partner have a relationship that isn't afraid of the truth? Read through the following questions. Think about them carefully. If you really want to get serious about having more honesty in your relationship, write down your answers and pray about who to share them with.

- Are there weaknesses in your life that you intentionally keep from your partner so the relationship can continue?

- Are there things you would like to do (date others, join a club) that you do not share with your partner so you can keep the relationship going?

- Are there controversial subjects you would like to talk about but you don't because you don't want to argue?

- Does your partner have weaknesses you would like to talk about but you don't because you're afraid he or she will come unglued?
- Are there certain concerns you have about the relationship that you're afraid to mention?

Another way to see if your dating relationship is "happy in the truth" is to think about what happens when you and your partner disagree. It's easy to get along when everything is going well. The real test comes when there's a disagreement. Here are five negative ways people deal with a problem in their relationship. Have you ever thought or acted in any of these ways?

- Refusing to talk about the problem.
- Making a big joke out of a serious situation.
- Pouting or sulking.
- Trying the silent treatment.
- Planning revenge, thinking *I'm going to get even later.*

All of us have been guilty of less-than-truthful communication at one time or another. However, our goal should be to build a relationship that isn't afraid of the truth. When we work through disagreements and hard times honestly, we often grow closer together. God isn't afraid of the truth, and we shouldn't be either.

It's a cliché, but it's true: "Honesty is the best policy." Love has nothing to hide. Love says let the chips fall where they will.

78

Not every relationship will survive, even when you have both been as honest as you can be. But I can promise you this: A relationship built on lies will *never* last.

There are times when an honest, truthful relationship should end. When that time comes, an honest partner won't try to back off in stages. That never works. The other person always catches on. If you want to break up, just do it. Cold turkey. Just remember to be kind and compassionate. Don't forget to ask God to help you be truthful, but gentle.

An old rock song from the sixties said, "Breaking up is hard to do." And it is. There will always be pain. Sometimes it's small, and sometimes it feels like your heart is going to explode. But a relationship that isn't afraid to face the truth, even when it means saying goodbye, can take comfort in knowing God was honored.

When it's over, thank God for the lessons you've learned. Thank Him that His principles about truthfulness protected both of you from committing yourselves to something that wasn't right. And thank Him that, because you were honest with each other, you can look back on your time together without guilt or regret.

9

Learning to Be Kind and Unselfish

I will know I am developing God's kind of loving relationship when . . . I am kind and unselfish toward my dating partner.

*L*ET'S AGAIN LOOK BACK AT 1 CORINTHIANS 13. True love, it says, is kind. True love, it says, "is not rude, is not selfish."

Let's take those in reverse order and discuss selfishness first. What does it mean to be selfish? Selfishness is an attitude that places my wants and needs above yours. It says "Me first" and "I want." When we are selfish we are sending a message to God that we don't trust Him to provide for our needs. We're out to provide them for ourselves.

I think everyone agrees that we live in a very selfish world. Everywhere you look it seems that people are consumed with making more, spending more, and buying more. Many seem to care only for themselves. All that they do appears to be motivated by selfishness.

Even as Christians, we have to constantly fight the temptation to act selfishly. With everyone around us looking out for number one, an attitude of selfishness hardly seems unusual.

But being selfish is about as far from God's kind of love as we can get. And it's a sure way to make a mess of your dating relationships. Whenever we begin to think that "me, my, and mine" are more important than you and yours, we are in trouble. The message we send is, "I can't really love you because I'm too busy taking care of myself."

Painful Lessons

In dating relationships selfish people may not realize how selfish they are being. They may believe that because they spend time and money to buy birthday and Christmas presents, they are somehow meeting their partners' needs.

Guess what? It just doesn't happen that way. Caring for another person the way God wants us to starts with *giving*. And that doesn't mean giving just our time or money. It means giving ourselves, our attention, our love, our caring. If you go into a relationship saying, "What can I get?" you really don't have a relationship; you've got an arrangement.

It goes like this: "I'll meet some of your needs if you meet some of mine. I'll give you two dates a week and a phone call every other day. In return, you give me compliments, companionship, sex, etc." The list can be endless. That's not a relationship; that's "Let's Make a Deal."

I'm convinced that thousands and thousands of students who think they have relationships are actually caught in selfish arrangements. When you are getting some of your needs met, it may feel like the other person really cares about you. But when a guy with a hot car and a big bank roll starts moving in, or when a girl with a big smile and a great personality shows up, does your dating partner still "care" about you or is he or she gone to the highest bidder? When an unwanted pregnancy comes along, does your boyfriend really care or does he bail out?

Selfishness and Sex

I know that sounds really cold, but there is nothing warm about selfishness. It can leave some deep and ugly scars.

I think it's also fair to say that in many, if not most cases, when a dating partner is selfish the pressure to have sex is greater. Selfish guys are especially guilty of pressuring girls to have sex. Their pitch often sounds like this: "If you give me sex, I'll make you feel loved. In fact, I'll promise you almost anything. But if you say no, then I'm gone."

Here's an excerpt from a letter I recently received that has "Let's Make a Deal" written between every line.

> My boyfriend and I are having some trouble. He wants me to move in with him. He wants me to do it with him. And he wants me to marry him. I told him that I can't. He says, "Why not? Your parents will forgive you." I don't know whether to break up with him. . . .

Did you have the same reaction to that letter as I did? When I first read it, I sat there yelling at the paper, "BREAK UP WITH HIM! BREAK UP WITH HIM!" as if she could hear me. She's being manipulated to the max, but she can't see it.

She needs to get out of Dodge and get as far away from that guy as she can. He's consumed by his own selfishness and doesn't give a flip about that girl. He had all kinds of "wants" for this girl, but I didn't see a single word about giving.

Another letter I received hammers home this thought even more. It's from a girl whose overwhelming need to be loved had driven her to some truly desperate deal-making:

> I wanted so much for someone to love me. And I would give a guy anything he wanted just so he would love me. But the biggest problem with this type of thinking, besides the obvious, is that for someone to really love me, I needed to give him nothing. If he loved me, he didn't need the extras and he wouldn't want them, either.

What a painful lesson she learned. Thank God she finally realized that real love doesn't come through deals and trade-offs.

How does your dating relationship compare with those we've just discussed? Are you and your partner giving or taking?

A Mark of Immaturity

Rudeness is a less deadly form of selfishness. All of us have had moments of rude behavior. Following is a list of some of the ways you can be rude in a dating relationship. Compare your actions to the ones on this list. Have you ever:

- Interrupted your partner while he or she is talking?

- Made fun of your date and hurt his or her feelings?
- Acted silly or obnoxious just to get attention?
- Looked away or quit listening while your partner was talking to you?
- Used bad language when you got angry?

Rudeness is simply a mark of immaturity. It is a form of demanding to be in the spotlight, for better or for worse. It is often a deliberate attempt to embarrass someone in revenge for something we think he or she has done to us.

The closer we become to someone, the greater our chances of being truly hurt. But rudeness is never an acceptable response to this hurt because it's basically a way to make the other person pay for hurting us. But real love does not keep score. It always seeks the best for the one we care for.

Love in Action

I don't think it takes a rocket scientist to figure out that God's kind of love always involves kindness. Kindness is the side of love that shows itself through giving. Kind people are always ready and willing to serve others. Ephesians 4:32 tells us to

Be kind and loving to each other, and forgive each other just as God forgave you in Christ.

Kindness concentrates on action. It just doesn't sit there. It does something.

That's where kindness fits into our love puzzle. Kindness is love in action. It will always find a way to give and to encourage. Kindness says "I will serve you. I will pay attention to your needs and try to meet them."

Kindness is hard work. That's because anytime you show your dating partner kindness, you have to think of your partner instead of yourself. Relationships that last are almost always characterized by lots of kindness. That means having a commitment to serve your partner as Christ serves you. In fact, Galatians 5:13 urges us to

Serve each other with love.

One major warning sign that a relationship is based on infatuation rather than love is that acts of kindness aren't consistent. They only happen every once in a while. A relationship fueled by infatuation starts to fizzle out and become boring when it becomes obvious that giving and caring are hard work. Then serving the other person becomes a pain instead of a pleasure.

Think about it. When you first begin dating a person you really like, isn't it easy to do kind, thoughtful things for him or her? But as the relationship continues, your acts of kindness may become less automatic. That's where real love kicks in and chooses to do kind things.

What are some of the ways you can show kindness in a dating relationship? How about:

- Being a patient listener?
- Looking for ways to give sincere compliments?
- Spending time with your dating partner's parents?

- Washing his or her car?
- Spending time learning about things that interest the other person?
- Making a big deal of birthdays?

A relationship is not based on real love unless you and your partner are willing to give kindness away and expect nothing in return.

10

Learning to Love without Conditions

I will know I am developing God's kind of loving relationship when . . . I reject the temptation to try and make my partner exactly what I want him or her to be.

*T*HINK FOR A MOMENT ABOUT SOME OF YOUR GOOD FRIENDS. Why do you get along so well with them? More than likely, it's because you accept each other just as you are. Neither of you puts conditions on your friendship. No one is under pressure to do certain things or behave in certain ways to be accepted. The truth is, you like one another for who you are.

You need to approach your dating relationships in much the same way. Now I'm not saying you shouldn't have standards. Much of this book is about developing biblical standards for who you date. By now it should be clear that your dating partners need to be growing Christians and they need to have a lifestyle that rejects sin and tries to obey the commands of Scripture.

I'm also not saying you shouldn't have preferences. It's obviously unwise to become serious about someone you can't get along with.

But God's kind of love says, "I'll accept you as you are. I love you unconditionally." On the other hand, infatuation will always try to change the personality or the lifestyle of a dating partner. Infatuation says, "You ought to do this. You ought to live like that."

Infatuation wants to change lots of things. Things like:

- You talk too much.
- You're too quiet.
- You never change your hair.
- You're never on time.
- You're lazy.
- You can't ever make up your mind.
- You wear funny clothes.
- You're selfish.
- You keep changing your mind.
- You're jealous.
- You get your feelings hurt too easily.
- You're too impatient.

The list goes on and on. That's because infatuation is a form of selfishness that does nothing to show love or encourage the other person.

Here are some other reasons why you shouldn't try to pressure someone into changing:

- It doesn't work!
- It's immature!
- It's not a characteristic of true love!

What's on Your List?

If someone is afraid of losing you, he or she may pretend to make a change you are asking for, but when the pressure is off, that person will go back to who he or she really is. In the end, you can't change someone through your own efforts. Real change in a person's life, including your dating partner, will only come from the inside through the guidance of the Holy Spirit.

When you try to force your partner to meet your own expectations, you are taking a big risk with that person's life. You may end up making him or her feel insecure, threatened, and in fear of being rejected. You can also damage your partner's self-image.

When you begin to date someone, you need to ask yourself this question: "Am I putting this person on a performance scale to see how he or she measures up to my own expectations, or am I accepting him or her unconditionally the way God accepted me?"

Here's a story to illustrate the point. This college guy (let's call him Aaron) called in to DAWSON McALLISTER LIVE! one night. Aaron had an incredible list of expectations for the woman he hoped to marry.

> I developed a list. Now this list just didn't deal with the physical aspects, but it dealt with the spiritual aspects too.
>
> I made it up myself. I definitely prayed about it . . . like the way she looked, the color of her hair, the color of her eyes. I got really technical on my list because I figured if I'm going to be with this girl, who I plan to marry and live with for the rest of my life, I want to be happy with her. And so I developed this list a long time ago.
>
> But then when I had been dating awhile, I

was thinking to myself, *I must be crazy. Because a lot of these girls I'm dating meet a lot of points on my list, but they don't meet everything.* And what I found myself starting to do was compromise.

This list is an advanced stage. I'm already past the criteria of 'she loves God and she's a Christian.' This list is really technical.

But it seemed impossible for any girl to meet the complete list. So I just decided to give it all over to God.

And guess what happened when Aaron went back to college after the summer!

"Lo and behold, there she was," he said.

So things worked out well for Aaron. But that didn't happen until he turned everything over to God. We must be very careful about doing what Aaron did. His "Miss Perfection" list almost ran him into a rut. Aaron's dates must have been something to watch too. I suspect he missed a lot of friendships and good times because he was so consumed with checking each of his dates against his huge list.

Another problem with having a list is that it doesn't always change with your own growth. Everyone goes through the process of changing and maturing. The perfect person today may not look quite as appealing tomorrow. Remember, God knows you better than you know yourself. Trust *Him* to keep the list!

Let's be honest. There aren't any perfect people out there for you to date. But that's good, because if there were, they would never be content with less-than-perfect you. That's one of the reasons God wants you to learn how to accept your dating partners just as they are, unconditionally.

Another reason to love unconditionally is that this kind of love has the best chance of growing deeper and stronger over the years. When we give love unconditionally, we are giving our partners a great gift. We are showing them that they don't have to be afraid of being rejected. And that's something that will bring incredible peace and freedom to our relationships.

This is exactly the message we find in 1 John 4:18–19:

Where God's love is, there is no fear, because God's perfect love drives out fear. It is punishment that makes a person fear, so love is not made perfect in the person who fears. We love because God first loved us.

As Christians, God values us all the same. He is patient with us no matter what our weaknesses. And best of all, He doesn't keep score when we fail. He forgives, He forgets, and He never uses our sins and mistakes against us.

When you show unconditional love toward the people you date, your relationships will be a lot more secure. That's why it's important for you to ask yourself this question if you think you may really be in love: "Could I live with this person, just the way he or she is right now, for the rest of my life?"

Real love can never be based on the fear that you must "perform" each day—or else. Successful, loving relationships are always based on God's unconditional love and acceptance.

11

Helping Your Partner Live for Christ

I will know I am developing God's kind of loving relationship when . . .
I am honestly trying to encourage my partner to be more like Jesus.

IN THE LAST CHAPTER, WE DISCUSSED HOW REAL LOVE IS UNCONDITIONAL, accepts people as they are, and does not try to change them into what we think they should be. But that doesn't mean people don't need to grow and change. After all, none of us is perfect. There is room to improve in all of our lives.

God clearly says that He wants us to encourage each other to be better Christians:

> **But encourage each other every day while it is "today." Help each other so none of you will become hardened because sin has tricked you.**
> **Heb. 3:13**

The thrill of sin can trick even the best Christian. No matter how strong your dating partner is, he or she still has spiritual struggles just like you. Don't pretend those struggles don't exist. The longer you ignore a sin, no matter how small, the more it becomes a habit. This is what Hebrews 3 means when it talks about becoming "hardened because [of] sin."

You and your partner need spiritual encouragement every day to help you avoid the tricks sin attempts to play on us all. If you are in a true, loving relationship, you and your partner will always be trying to help each other grow closer to Jesus.

Creative Ways to Encourage
Spiritual Growth

I've already said this earlier in the book, but I want to say it again. Having a good date life shouldn't be your top priority. Finding the person you will marry shouldn't be your top priority. Your top priority should be to love God and become more and more like Jesus Christ.

Part of God's intention for your date life is that you provide spiritual encouragement to the people you date. In fact, true love's first concern is that the other person will grow spiritually. Accomplishing that takes a little planning.

Think about the kinds of activities you and your dating partner do together for fun. Do you: study? ride bikes? go to the zoo? play sports? take walks? take a drive? cook? shop? go to movies? go out to eat? ride horses? go to church?

Have you ever thought about doing things together that can help each other grow spiritually, such as:

- Asking each other how you are doing spiritually?
- Studying the Bible together?
- Memorizing Bible verses?
- Praying each time you are together?
- Sharing your faith with a mutual friend?
- Working on a missions project?

- Visiting a nursing home?
- Leading a Bible study together?
- Reading a good book together?

Thinking of creative ways to help each other grow as Christians is an important part of a healthy, loving relationship.

Yes, it will take some effort, but nurturing real love will always include some hard work. One thing's for sure: If you are simply infatuated with your partner, you will never be disciplined enough or interested enough to do these things.

Here are several questions for you to think about:

- What are you and your partner currently doing together to grow spiritually?

- How often do you talk about spiritual things when you are together?

- What was the last thing you did to encourage your dating partner to live for Christ?

- What was the last thing your dating partner did to encourage you to live for Christ?

- How do you think you could do better at being a spiritual encourager?

Now you need to think carefully about how you answered these questions. Are there any clues indicating that one or both of you are not being the kind of spiritual encourager that real love requires? If so, you may need to work on this area of your relationship.

None of us is perfect, but if you don't have a real passion to see your dating partner live for Christ, then it's time to examine yourself and the relationship.

The Godly Heart

Real love requires that you seek Christian dating partners who are serious about God, who will help you be serious about God, and who you want to help to be more serious about God. If you settle for less, one of the deepest needs you have—to love and worship God together—will go unmet.

Ladies, a guy with a heart for God will be just as concerned about your heart for God. Guys, the same is true in reverse. A girl with a heart for God will never be content unless your heart is committed to Christ as hers is. Of course, this doesn't mean you shouldn't be physically attracted to each other too. You should be. But it should never be at the expense of what's in your heart.

In the Old Testament book of 1 Samuel, there is a great example of how important a godly heart is. God sent Samuel to Jesse, a man with eight sons. One of those sons was God's choice to be the new king over Israel, but He had not told Samuel which son it was. So Samuel contacted Jesse and invited him and his family to a sacrifice where the new king would be appointed. Here's what happened:

> **When they arrived, Samuel saw Eliab, and he thought, "Surely the LORD has appointed this person standing here before him." But the LORD said to Samuel, "Don't look at how handsome Eliab is or how tall he**

is, because I have not chosen him. God does
not see the same way people see. People look
at the outside of a person, but the LORD looks
at the heart."

1 Sam. 16:6–7

The most important quality anyone can have is a
warm heart for God.

When both of you have such a heart, God can do
awesome things in your lives. Each of you will motivate
the other to have a deeper walk with God. And you will
be willing to work at your relationships with God and
with each other.

When that happens, watch out! As together, you
grow more and more like Christ, you'll also become
better "lovers." After all, a heart filled with Christ is
love's best teacher.

12

Avoiding Jealousy

*I will know I am developing
God's kind of loving
relationship when . . .
I am not jealous or
possessive.*

*I*F YOU TALK HONESTLY ABOUT THE LOVE PUZZLE, you can't leave out the big, fat, ugly piece called *jealousy*. If you want a way to wreck a dating relationship, just start getting possessive.

Hey, don't take my word for it; take God's:

Where jealousy and selfishness are, there will be confusion and every kind of evil.

James 3:16

The Bible doesn't pull any punches. If you or your dating partner are jealous or possessive, then there will be trouble in your relationship, and you will be the cause of it.

So what are jealousy and possessiveness? Jealousy is a negative emotion. It is actually a form of selfishness. When you are jealous, you want to be the focus of your partner's attention most if not all of the time. When your dating partner spends time with someone else, jealousy may cause you to be hurt and angry. When you act out your jealousy by trying to keep your dating partner from doing anything that isn't done with you, it's called being possessive.

Struggling against Jealousy

Jealousy is like a weed that takes over in our heart. The larger it grows, the more it crowds out real love. First Corinthians 13:4 makes the difference between love and jealousy very clear when it says,

Love is not jealous.

So let's think about the difference between love and jealousy a moment. Let's imagine that you are struggling with jealousy right now. Every time your dating partner chooses to spend time doing something besides being with you, you don't like it. In fact, you don't even like him or her to talk to anyone else. You really don't trust this person very much, do you? You're worried he or she may start to have doubts about your relationship. You start experiencing feelings of rejection and anger just thinking about this possibility.

So what do you think your struggle with jealousy reveals about the condition of your dating relationship? Let me suggest an answer: It probably indicates you are not experiencing true love. It probably means you are simply infatuated.

Infatuation is easily threatened, so it is always jealous and insecure. Infatuation is usually more concerned about what it can get out of a relationship than what it has to give to make things work. People who are caught up in infatuation want to be the focus of the other person's complete attention. So they become upset when some of that attention gets spent on other people or activities.

Can you see why this is so damaging to a relationship? It's like putting this person you supposedly care about into a little prison. Your jealousy attempts to take away his or her choices and freedom. Jealousy makes you expect this person to meet your needs at the expense of his or her own needs. This is obviously a very selfish attitude.

Dating partners never have the right to cut off other relationships in each other's life. Doing that would deprive them of activities and people who could make incredible differences in their lives. Moreover, if you try to hang on too hard, your partner will begin to feel trapped. When that happens, it is only a matter of time before he or she decides to escape from the prison your jealousies built.

Now you may be thinking, "That's great, Dawson, but what do I do when some other girl is flirting with my guy?" or "What do I do when another guy begins hitting on my girl?"

I know what usually happens: hate stares, the silent treatment, cutting remarks. Everybody's friends choose sides and the war can go on for days and even weeks.

But let me ask you a question: Who wins? The answer is pretty obvious, but I'm going to say it anyway: NOBODY! And especially not love.

The very moment you begin to sense jealousy in your own life, you need to stop and remember that the choice to be jealous is yours and yours alone. And you need to remember that where jealousy plays nobody wins. It's immature. It's selfish. It will not make your relationship better, but it will almost certainly cause some real damage. And most important, remember that real love, God's kind of love, is not jealous.

Think about this: Real love wants what is best for the other person. Real love says, "I care about you so much that I give you complete freedom to develop into whoever God wants you to be. I want you to make the best choices for your life no matter how it affects me or our relationship."

If your love is a mature love, it will give your partner that kind of freedom and it will strengthen the respect and friendship between you. It doesn't guarantee a perfect love life, but it will lead to fewer bumps on the journey.

I want to make one other point before we move on. Your boyfriend or girlfriend is not now and never will be your possession. You do not own him or her. That person belongs to God. The time he or she spends with you in a dating relationship is a gift from God to you. When you forget that, your relationships will head off in the wrong direction. That's why God has given us such a firm reminder as this:

> **My dear brothers and sisters, do not be fooled about this. Every good action and every perfect gift is from God.**
> **James 1:16–17**

God Hates Jealousy

Since our relationships are gifts from God, He hates it when we are jealous and possessive with those gifts. Here are three reasons why this is true.

To begin with, God hates jealousy because it is an insulting way to treat a gift He has given us. Instead of caring for God's gift with gratitude, we are attempting to hold on to it by force. It's like shaking our fist at God and saying, "I deserve this, so don't ever try to take it away from me!"

This attitude hurts God deeply. After all, He knows every single need we have. He knows exactly what is best for us. And He gets tremendous pleasure in not only meeting our needs, but in being truly generous. When God gives us the opportunity for a warm dating relationship, He does it because He loves us, not because we've done anything to earn it. We don't deserve it, and God isn't obligated to give it.

Secondly, God hates jealousy because it damages and sometimes destroys the opportunity He has given us to serve another person and help that person grow in Christ. Mark 9:35 says,

Whoever wants to be the most important must be last of all and servant of all.

God's command for us to serve one another is very serious. Christ spent His whole ministry serving others. It is one of the most important jobs a Christian has. And the more time we spend with someone, as in a dating relationship, the more important our service to him or her becomes.

In contrast, when we become jealous we stop serving the other person and start serving only ourselves. Instead of helping your dating partner become the best he or she can be in Christ, when you are jealous you possessively try to limit your partner's rights. In fact, you do your partner harm by trying to selfishly control him or her. That is not God's way of loving. God tells us that a servant never takes advantage of the one he serves:

When you do things, do not let selfishness or pride be your guide. Instead, be

humble and give more honor to others than to yourselves. Do not be interested only in your own life, but be interested in the lives of others.

Phil. 2:3–4

The third reason God hates jealousy is that it often leads to selfish actions that hurt others as well as ourselves. Jealousy causes us to take our attention away from God and our friends so that we can focus it completely on ourselves. It causes us to do things we would not normally do.

If you have ever struggled with jealousy, think back on that time. What were you thinking? How did you act? Jealousy is not an easy thing to hide. It makes you suspicious of everyone. And in the end, it hurts you most of all. Proverbs 14:30 tells us that

Peace of mind means a healthy body, but jealousy will rot your bones.

13

Obeying God's Counsel about Sex

I will know I am developing God's kind of loving relationship when . . . I obey God's counsel about sex.

*M*ANY PEOPLE TODAY ARE SAYING THINGS LIKE, "The old ways just aren't good enough anymore. Throw them away. Things aren't done the way they used to be done. Bring in the new—that's what works today."

Well, here's my opinion: Not everything that's new works, and not everything that's old should be thrown away. And this is especially true when it comes to God's counsel about sex.

Do you think the Bible is old-fashioned, out-of-date stuff—that it doesn't work for us today, that it's just not practical?

Here's what I believe: If we toss God's truth into the trash can and buy into what the world is telling us about sex, our chances of having some major tragedies in our love lives are almost 100 percent. Without God's Word as our guide, we're almost guaranteed to wind up with a lot of cheap imitations of the real thing. And with those imitations will come incredible pain and hurt.

Do I sound pretty serious about this subject? You bet I do! If you don't care what God says about love and sex, you might as well trash this book right now. God's counsel about sex—just like His counsel on everything else—is the final word about the subject.

Think about it. How many times already in this book have we talked about God being the very author of love? He *is* love. He teaches us how to love. If we cut Him out of our love lives, we cut out love.

Remember also that God created us. His advice is always based on what He knows is best for us, even when we can't see it or understand it. If we will commit to following His laws, they never hurt us; they help us.

Unfortunately, many students have already made some serious mistakes involving sex. If you are in this situation, don't despair. God loves you as much as He ever did. If you're in this group, jump ahead and read chapter 16 in this book right now. It was written especially to you. You can come back to this chapter later.

A World of Confusing Messages

As we said earlier, when it comes to sex, the world is full of confusing messages, especially for students. Christians and a few others talk about abstinence, that is, not having sex until you're married. A few others say, "Go for it. Whatever feels good, do it!" Most are saying, "Have sex, just make it safe sex."

WHOA! STOP! There is no such thing as "safe sex" except with your husband or wife who was a virgin when you were married. Anybody can catch AIDS. The HIV virus is so small it can go right through a condom. And even if you don't catch AIDS, you have a really good chance of getting some other sexually transmitted disease. If you escape these, there's the possibility of pregnancy. There are also emotional scars from having sex before marriage, scars that may be with you for the rest of your life. And there can be other consequences from ignoring God's counsel about sex.

One thing is sure. A lot of Christian students are very confused about their sexuality, but they aren't willing to obey God's teaching on the subject. Take for instance the girl who wrote me the following letter:

> Hello. I have question concerning an issue in my life right now.
>
> OK, I have always heard you preach about pre-marital sex and how horrible it is. Well, I am 17 years old and I'm dating a 27-year-old guy right now, and that issue is everyone's primary concern with us.
>
> Almost everyone who knows about us has told me that he just wants sex from me, but that's not true. He's a Christian also and he knows it's against the Bible, but he is human. He has desires just like everyone else. So do I.
>
> My problem is this: We both care about each other a lot! And right now the way I feel about him, yes, I would have sex with him and he wouldn't have to pressure me at all.
>
> Since we're both Christians, we really care about each other. It wouldn't be a one-night stand. It would be out of true love.
>
> Even though this is our situation, my youth pastor is all over my case about how wrong that is. But why? My boyfriend wouldn't dump me; I know that. It would just be our true act of love for each other. Is that wrong? I know it's against the Bible, but I really love him!
>
> I have thoughts about it all the time and my friends tell me that's lustful and it's the same as doing it. Is that true? I need some answers because I don't want to cause any friction as a Christian but my hormones and heart say yes now.

118

Her hormones and her heart were telling her, "Yes. Go for it." God's counsel and her Christian friends were telling her, "No! Wait! Time out!" Who do you think she's going to listen to?

I don't know the answer to that, but I do know this: Sex will have a strong and powerful impact on your life. Even your relationship with God will be greatly influenced by what you think about sex and how you deal with your strong sex drive.

And I know one thing more: The Bible doesn't stutter on the matter of sex. It gives clear commands. And following those commands will bring you the greatest joy, the greatest pleasure, and the most fulfilling love you can possibly have.

Because sex is such a powerful force in dating relationships, we are going to discuss different aspects of it not only in this chapter but also in the three that follow. I'll begin by asking some important questions that I would like you to answer based on your current views of sex. The more honestly you answer, the more you'll benefit from the following chapters.

- How far sexually do you think you should go on a date?

- Do you think sex before marriage is wrong? Why?

- Do you believe sex before marriage is OK under certain conditions? Which conditions? Check all that apply:

    ____*When it helps you understand how you really feel about a person.*

____*When the two of you are planning to be married soon.*

____*When you want to learn how to be better lovers in marriage.*

____*When you want to have intercourse to decide whether you and your date are compatible.*

____*Other* _____

- Do you think fantasizing about sex is a healthy habit? Why?

- Do you believe sex should only be used for the purpose of having children? Why?

As we talk about some of these questions in the remaining pages of this book, I want you to keep two things in mind.

First, recognize that our sex drives are designed by God to be very strong. Experiencing these impulses is not sin. In fact, God has given them to us as a gift. The key is to keep these urges under control until the right time. Sex drives that are unleashed before God designed them to be can become a very destructive force, tearing up our lives and the lives of people around us.

Second, what the Bible says about sex was written to protect us. Remember that . . .

All Scripture is given by God and is useful for teaching, for showing people what is wrong in their lives, for correcting faults, and for teaching how to live right. Using the Scriptures, the person who serves God will be capable, having all that is needed to do every good work.

2 Tim. 3:16–17

120

Sex Was God's Idea

When two people of the opposite sex are involved physically—from holding hands to sexual intercourse—they're usually looking for more than just physical stimulation. Behind their physical actions are deep emotional needs such as love, acceptance, security, and attention. They want those needs met.

And those internal needs are normal. We all desire to love and be loved. But we have to realize that when our emotional needs get mixed up with our sex drives, even more intense desires are created.

On top of this, the rest of the world seems to have gone crazy over sex. Notice all the advertisements that use sex to sell things. Between the advertisements, television, and the movies, we are being fed a very perverted view of what sex is all about.

In light of this flood of misinformation it is desperately important for us to hear and understand God's perspective on sex.

Remember: God is the Creator of all things, including sex. He designed us with strong sex drives. It was not an afterthought, not something He came up with at the last minute. It was a vital part of His plan and creation. God wants married people to have total sexual fulfillment.

The Bible says,

> **So God created human beings in his image. In the image of God he created them. He created them male and female. God blessed them and said, "Have many children and grow in number. Fill the earth and be its master. Rule over the fish in the sea and over the birds in the sky and over every living thing that**

moves on the earth." . . . God looked at
everything he had made, and it was very good.
Gen. 1:27–28, 31

Jesus Christ also approved of sex. One of the stories
from His public ministry indicates this.

> Some Pharisees came to Jesus and tried to
> trick him. They asked, "Is it right for a man to
> divorce his wife for any reason he chooses?"
> Jesus answered, "Surely you have read in the
> Scriptures: When God made the world, 'he
> made them male and female.' And God said,
> 'So a man will leave his father and mother and
> be united with his wife, and the two people
> will become one body.' So there are not two,
> but one. God has joined the two people to-
> gether, so no one should separate them."
> Matt. 19:3–6

The Bible also makes it clear that God created sex for
more than the purpose of having children. He also designed it for the purpose of pleasure. While sexual intercourse in marriage is a truly holy event, God intended it
to be tremendously enjoyable. Look at what Proverbs
says about sexual pleasure between a husband and wife:

> May your fountain be blessed, and may
> you rejoice in the wife of your youth. A loving
> doe, a graceful deer—may her breasts satisfy you
> always, may you ever be captivated by her love.
> Why be captivated, my son, by an adulteress?
> Why embrace the bosom of another man's wife?
> Prov. 5:18–20 NIV

God wants married people, united in Him, to enjoy each other's body. He has uniquely made the human body for His glory and for the enjoyment of a marriage partner. God's goal for married couples is to experience fulfillment from each other's love and physical appearance. That's why Scripture states,

> **Each man should have his own wife, and each woman should have her own husband. The husband should give his wife all that he owes her as his wife. And the wife should give her husband all that she owes him as her husband. The wife does not have full rights over her own body; her husband shares them. And the husband does not have full rights over his own body; his wife shares them. Do not refuse to give your bodies to each other, unless you both agree to stay away from sexual relations for a time so you can give your time to prayer. Then come together again so Satan cannot tempt you because of a lack of self-control.**
>
> **1 Cor. 7:2–5**

God has made it very clear that He wants our marriages to include the most exciting and enjoyable sex possible. It's an awesome wedding gift from God directly to us.

However, sex outside of marriage is no gift at all. In the next chapter we will look at some of the reasons why this is so and what the Bible says about avoiding premarital sex.

14

The Destructive Power of Premarital Sex

I will know I am developing God's kind of loving relationship when . . . my dating partner and I clearly understand the destructive power of sex outside of marriage.

*I*N THE LAST CHAPTER, WE SAW HOW GOD VIEWS SEX, how He created sex, and how He wants us to enjoy it within marriage. It's a great plan, but it creates another problem. How do we keep our strong sex drives under control for several years before we get married?

One thing is certain: Satan wants to convince us that we are controlled by our glands. He has filled our world with the destructive lie that our passions are the most important thing in our lives. His message is simple: "Hey, if you want it, do it. If you feel like having sex, go for it."

Satan, like God, fully understands how destructive sex can be when it is misused. He knows that sex can unleash powerful emotions that feel like love and are very addictive. And he knows that once we've experienced the addictive closeness of sex, it will be much harder for us to resist it in the future.

That is why God has given us His commands about sexual purity. He's not trying to make things difficult for us; He's trying to protect us from the addictive power of sex. So what does God have to say about premarital sex?

God wants you to be holy and to stay away from sexual sins. He wants each of you

to learn to control your own body in a way that is holy and honorable. Don't use your body for sexual sin like the people who do not know God.

1 Thess. 4:3–5

Avoiding Difficult Temptations

There is a godly way to deal with our sexuality and there is a sinful way. A lot of that has to do with the kinds of temptations we expose ourselves to.

One of the common ways Christian students create difficult temptations for themselves is by dating non-Christians. Or as the Scripture put it, dating "people who do not know God" and therefore are far more likely to use their bodies "for sexual sin."

Non-Christians will often want things from the relationship that you don't want to give. And they may not care about anything else.

Becca understands that. She called into DAWSON McALLISTER LIVE! one Sunday night and told her story on nationwide radio. She had been dating the same guy for about a year. One night, he asked her straight out to have sex with him. She told him she wasn't ready—and wouldn't be until marriage. He insisted they were ready, that they had a good relationship.

When Becca responded by sharing her belief that sex is wrong outside of marriage, here's the way the radio conversation went:

> Becca: My boyfriend said, "Where did you get that foolish garbage?" And I

started telling him why God said it is
wrong, and he was sitting there like,
"Don't preach at me. This isn't what I
want to hear."

Dawson: Yeah, he thought he was going to get
some action and all he got was a
sermon. I bet he was ticked.

Becca and her boyfriend broke up soon after that.
And it's good they did. Once he found out that the only
thing Becca was going to give him was a sermon, he
moved on. And it's no secret where he's going. He'll
find another girl who will have sex with him.

Becca's boyfriend called God's Word "foolish gar-
bage." And to him it is. Becca made the mistake of
dating a non-Christian to begin with, but thankfully she
was able to resist temptation when it attacked. She did it
by thinking like God thinks. And God's thoughts are
that we are to avoid any activity that involves the misuse of sex.

**But there must be no sexual sin among
you, or any kind of evil or greed. Those
things are not right for God's holy people.**
Eph. 5:3

Why does God give us such strict guidelines
against love-play and sex when we are dating? Why
does He lovingly tell us to save it for marriage?

The thrill of sexual arousal can make someone feel
loved, accepted, secure, and especially close to his or her
partner. And sometimes when those needs are strong,

we run recklessly into someone's arms wanting him or her to meet those needs. For a few moments we feel safe and secure and think our needs have been met. But just like the sex act itself, those feelings of safety and security are short-lived. As soon as they've faded away, our unmet needs come flooding back.

There's a story in the Old Testament about a man named Amnon who believed he was desperately in love with a beautiful virgin named Tamar. His emotions were strong, powerfully strong. In fact, they were out of control. She suggested they get married. This is what happened next:

> **But Amnon refused to listen to her. He was stronger than she was, so he forced her to have sexual relations with him. After that, Amnon hated Tamar. He hated her more than he had loved her before. Amnon said to her, "Get up and leave!" . . . He called his young servant back in and said, "Get this woman out of here and away from me! Lock the door after her." So his servant led her out of the room and bolted the door after her.**
>
> **2 Sam. 13:14–15, 17–18**

What an amazing and terrible change. When Amnon had finished his few moments of passion, what he thought was love turned instantly into hate. Unfortunately, this kind of one-night stand is still with us today as those driven by lust and selfishness continue to leave a disastrous trail of broken hearts and damaged spirits.

An Emotional Disaster

Sex without love and marriage is nothing but a cheap, deceptive imitation. And it almost always leads to pain and heartbreak.

A while back, I received a letter from a girl we'll call Michelle. She was a pastor's daughter, a virgin, and had had little more than a few good-night kisses. She was only thirteen years old. One evening she met an older guy. He gave her a back rub. But like Amnon, he had more on his mind. One thing led to another. Here's part of her painful story:

> Well, I know I wasn't raped, but he did stuff to me I never would have done, ever, if we had been dating. He took advantage of me and I feel really bad.
>
> Why did he have to choose me to get his thrills off of? Why me?
>
> And he never even looked at me once. He never kissed me. It was all for him.
>
> Now, whenever I'm around a guy, I get all tight inside and I'm scared. Even if the guy is just a friend or if it's someone that I really think is cute and I really like, I get all tense when that guy touches me, even if it's just on my back or somewhere "safe."

What a tragedy. She's only thirteen, and already she carries a scar that will take many years to fade.

Stick to God's Game Plan

The Bible is clear: Sex is not love. Without the love and commitment of marriage, sex between two people is an emotional disaster. Even if you could completely protect yourself against disease, which you can't, there would still be no such thing as safe sex before marriage. You know why? Because you can't protect your emotions or your mind or your soul. There's no such thing as a condom to cover your heart!

God is neither cruel nor uncaring. His commands concerning sex are both wise and loving. He longs for each of us to have the incredible pleasure of becoming true lovers within stable marriages. And the best chance for that to happen is if we stick to His game plan and don't start trying to call our own plays.

That means you have to develop self-control now. Actually, teaching self-control is one of the ways God protects your future marriage. After all, if you can't control your sexual urges now, there's a much greater chance of failing to do so after you are married. Can you imagine how awful you would feel to wake up and discover that the man or woman of your dreams is now dreaming of someone else?

Staying Sexually Pure

Before we finish this chapter, there is one more thing we need to discuss about the misuse of sex. More than anything else, it is a symptom of a spiritual problem.

A little while ago, a girl we'll call Kelly called into DAWSON McALLISTER LIVE! She said her friends were pressuring her to have sex.

Kelly was a virgin. She told her friends she believed premarital sex was wrong and she was going to wait until she was married. I am really proud of her for that.

But I also wanted to make sure she understood that her friends' decision to experiment with sex was more than just a bad decision. It was an indication that they had real spiritual needs.

In other words, her friends' major problem was that they did not know Christ.

I told Kelly she must continue to be strong in her commitment to stay sexually pure, but that she must also continue to clearly tell her friends why she was making that choice. She needs to tell her friends that obeying God's commands about sex protects her. And she needs to let them know that she made a commitment to obey God's commands when she put her faith in Christ. Then I gave her this verse to share with them:

> **So run away from sexual sin. Every other sin people do is outside their bodies, but those who sin sexually sin against their own bodies. You should know that your body is a temple for the Holy Spirit who is in you. You have received the Holy Spirit from God. So you do not belong to yourselves, because you were bought by God for a price. So honor God with your bodies.**
> **1 Cor. 6:18–20**

The best reason of all to say no to the misuse of sex is love and respect for God. He never lies to us. He is constantly working to protect us. And He is always ready to forgive us when we fail. We owe it to God to honor Him by staying sexually pure. When you wait until marriage to have sex, God will bless you with more love and security and excitement and pleasure than you can imagine.

15

Setting Sexual Standards

I will know I am developing God's kind of loving relationship when . . . my partner and I decide, with God's direction, how far sexually we will allow the relationship to go.

THROUGHOUT THIS BOOK WE HAVE TALKED ABOUT HOW THE WORLD IS FULL OF CONFUSION about love and sex. We've discussed how Satan lies to us when it comes to our sexuality. And we've seen how incredibly deceptive hc can be.

For example, Satan works overtime to keep us thinking about sex, but we seldom give a thought to the fifteen-year-old girl delivering her baby alone because her boyfriend has long since abandoned her. We almost never hear about couples who thought they were sharing love but wound up sharing a sexually transmitted disease.

It's a sure thing that Satan doesn't want us to see the ugly side of what happens when we misuse sex. His deceptions are very subtle. And we are easily deceived.

God hates those deceptions. He wants us to have the wisdom to avoid them. And nowhere do you need God's wisdom more than in how you handle sex in your dating relationships.

We've seen how God is against premarital sex or heavy premarital love-play. (Look back at 1 Thess. 4:3–6.) But there's a question we haven't discussed: How far sexually should you allow your dating relationships to go?

What Really Counts

There is something you must understand before we begin to study this. The Bible does not spell out a list of specific rules or instructions to tell you how far you should go. It doesn't say you should stop at holding hands or hugging or kissing. However, God does give clear commands and powerful principles that He wants you to apply to this part of your dating life. Unfortunately, a lot of students choose to ignore them.

I talked with a girl recently who told me she depends on her emotions, on how she feels, to dictate how far she should go with her dates. In other words, if it feels right she's gonna do it. TIME OUT! Don't ever trust your emotions to make any decision for you. We've already talked about this in more than one chapter of this book. Your standards must go far deeper than how you feel or what you're comfortable with.

Feelings are like the weather—they may change at any moment.

I did my best to explain this to her. I told her that what counts is not what she feels or what he feels. What counts is what God says. I told her that if we really want to walk with God, our goal in life must be to obey God. And to obey God, we must understand that emotions can trick us but God always tells us the truth.

Listen to what David said about God's counsel in Psalm 119:98–100:

Your commands make me wiser than my enemies, because they are mine forever. I am wiser than all my teachers, because I think about your rules. I have more understanding

than the older leaders, because I follow your orders.

The Bible very clearly tells us that God's commands will make us wiser in two ways. They make us wiser than our enemies (Satan, who lies to us; the world, which encourages us to do whatever we feel; and our ourselves—that is, our natural selfishness that by itself has no standards at all).

God's commands also make us wiser than our teachers. Our teachers can be anybody we take advice from, and that advice can be good or bad. It should always be checked against what God has to say on the subject.

Here's a story about a couple who accepted God's plan for becoming wiser. One night during my radio show, I got a call from a guy who was getting married soon. He told me that he and his fiancé had discussed the issue of sex in their relationship right from the start.

Before anything happened, my fiancé and I sat down and calmly and coolly set down guidelines. We set guidelines according to what we believed were morally right standards according to God's Word.

We decided that we could hold hands and kiss and hug, but if we got to the point where the temptation got too great for us to continue kissing and made us go past our moral guidelines, we would have to stop.

It's not an easy thing at all, but it can be done. We've had to work very hard.

I think it's important to understand that even though this couple used God's commands and principles to help them set standards, they still found it was hard work. There was plenty of temptation for them to give in. But they didn't. They stuck to their decision, they relied on God's standards, and the result was a pure and God-honoring relationship all the way to their wedding day.

Let's compare that story to the radio conversation I had with a fifteen-year-old girl who, after dating a nineteen-year-old guy for almost five months, lost her virginity. Here's what she said to me:

> I just wanted to say watch out, because how far is too far? It can be the very minute your boyfriend gets you alone . . .

During our conversation she admitted to becoming confused. Little by little, she had allowed her older boyfriend to push her into sex. He messed with her head and then he messed with her body.

Guess what? They never talked about standards. They didn't pay any attention to God's commands. And this poor girl found out that ignoring God can be painful.

That's why talking about how far you should go is so important in your dating relationships. Both partners must come to an agreement that is based on God's principles.

However, it's important that you don't come at this discussion the wrong way. You should not be talking about how far you can go without sinning. The real issue is, "Let's be sure the physical side of our relationship honors God and protects each other."

Principles for a Sexually Pure Relationship

So far in this chapter we've looked at how several couples have either protected or destroyed their sexual purity. Now it's time to learn the principles that will enable you to obey God, protect your relationships, and keep yourself sexually pure.

1. The "I Will Only Date Christians" Principle

This principle was covered in detail in chapter 4, so we won't spend much more time on it here. But I want to be very clear on this: It is almost impossible to set godly sexual standards with a non-Christian. As a Christian you're looking at your relationship from God's point of view. Non-Christians aren't. Violating this principle causes trouble the moment the date begins.

2. The "I Will Only Date Christians Who Are a Good Spiritual Influence on Me" Principle

This principle is covered in detail in chapter 5, so again we won't spend much more time on it here. We'll cut to the bottom line: Christians who don't live what they say they believe are living like non-Christians. There is almost no difference between dating non-Christians and dating Christians who are not walking with God. If they aren't obeying God in other areas of their lives, they probably won't obey God's commands about sexuality.

140

3. The Self-Control Principle

There is no question that the temptation to experiment with sex can be incredibly powerful. Sexual urges are so strong, it's hard to imagine that anyone else has ever experienced so much temptation. But those urges affect everyone. We can take courage and inspiration from the Bible, which tells us that Jesus once faced a time of temptation that was far greater than any we will ever have to face. And He overcame them.

"Then the Spirit led Jesus into the desert to be tempted by the devil. Jesus ate nothing for forty days and nights. After this, he was very hungry. The devil came to Jesus to tempt him, saying, 'If you are the Son of God, tell these rocks to become bread' " (Matt. 4:1–3).

There are greater physical needs than sex. One of them is hunger. We can live without sex but we cannot live without food. Catch this: Jesus had not eaten for forty days and nights. Can you even imagine how hungry He was? His desire to eat was a greater physical need than most of us have ever felt.

So Satan tempted Jesus to use His power to turn stones to bread. On first thought, it seems like a reasonable thing for Christ to do. After all, He was starving and certainly had the power to create some food. But Jesus responded to Satan's challenge by saying this: **"It is written in the Scriptures, 'A person does not live by eating only bread, but by everything God says' "** (Matt 4:4).

The Scripture Jesus was quoting is in Deuteronomy 8:3 in the Old Testament. This verse tells us the story of the children of Israel who wandered in the desert for forty years. Each day, God provided them with special food (manna) so they could survive. God in His love and power was teaching them to rely on Him to meet their most basic needs.

When Satan tempted Jesus to turn stones into bread, he was actually challenging Jesus to ignore God's promise that He would meet all His needs. He was tempting Jesus to meet His own needs and forget God.

Jesus was desperate for food. But He knew that by taking matters into His own hands He would be disobeying God. He also knew that God would give Him all the self-control He needed. Knowing these things, Jesus was able to forcefully tell Satan that God had promised to totally provide for Him. He resisted Satan's temptation so He could receive God's very best.

In the same way Satan tempted Jesus, he wants you to believe you should meet your own needs instead of depending on God. He knows your selfish attempts to fulfill your own sexual desires will hurt you severely. And when that happens, Satan wins. God wants you to depend on Him now for the self-control you need to avoid Satan's temptation. And He wants you to depend on Him in the future until He brings you sexual fulfillment inside of a godly marriage.

God wants you to know that we are not like animals with no self-control. He wants us to know that we are new creatures in Christ who have the power, the self-control, to wait for Him to give us His very best.

4. The "Selfish-Touch" Principle

In 1 Corinthians, the apostle Paul wrote, **"Now concerning the things about which you wrote, it is good for a man not to touch a woman"** (1 Cor. 7:1 NASB). In the context of this verse, the word *touch* is a powerful

142

word. It means to touch someone in a way that arouses his or her sexual desire and emotional needs. If a guy touches a girl in a way that arouses her passion, he has acted selfishly and has gone too far.

5. The "Sex Controls the Date" Principle

Another verse in 1 Corinthians says, " 'I am allowed to do all things,' but all things are not good for me to do. 'I am allowed to do all things,' but I will not let anything make me its slave" (1 Cor. 6:12). God does not want our lives to be controlled or enslaved by anything or anyone but Him. If the physical part of a relationship is controlling your time together, then you've gone too far. Ask yourself this question: If we took all physical activity away from our date life, would there be enough left to keep that relationship going?

6. The "Sex Controls My Thoughts" Principle

God does not want your mind constantly dwelling on passion and sex. He tells us in Colossians 3:5 to "put all evil things out of your life: sexual sinning, doing evil, letting evil thoughts control you, wanting things that are evil, and greed. This is really serving a false god." If what you do on a date causes you or your partner to fantasize about inappropriate sexual activity, you have gone too far.

7. The "Does It Cause Me to Mislead?" Principle

Any kind of sexual activity can lead your dating partner to believe you are more serious and committed than you really are. Ephesians 4:25 says, **"So you must stop telling lies. Tell each other the truth, because we all belong to each other in the same body."** If your physical activity on a date misleads your partner about how much you really care, you are not being honest and you have gone too far.

8. The "Protect Your Future Husband or Wife" Principle

You may not yet have dated or even met your future marriage partner. There's a good chance your future partner is dating someone else right now. Think about this: How far do you want your future mate going in his or her sexual activity right now? How far do you think your future mate wants you to be going in your sexual activity right now?

9. The "Good-Memories" Principle

Here are some of the simplest but most powerful words the apostle Paul ever spoke: **"I thank my God every time I remember you"** (Phil. 1:3). Can you say that about the people you have dated in the past? Can they say that about you? If you do not go too far in your dating relationships, when those relationships end you will always be able to have a clear conscience, knowing you treated those people with honesty and respect, as God commands.

There's no question that God has a lot to say on the subject of sexual purity. He wants to help you set standards that really work. But for that to happen, you need to set those standards before the first good-night kiss.

16

It's Never Too Late to Be Sexually Pure

I will know I am developing God's kind of loving relationshp when . . .
I commit to obeying God's commands about love and sex, even though I have failed in the past.

I KNOW THAT SOME OF YOU HAVE ALREADY BLOWN IT when it comes to sex. You've already gone too far and you know it. You may have even turned to this chapter before reading any other. In fact, I hope you did, because you may be wondering, "Is there anything in this book for me, or is it already too late?"

Here's my answer: *It's never too late to be sexually pure! It's never too late to ask God to forgive you. And it's never too late to forgive yourself.* The Bible is clear that God loves you, He wants to forgive you, and He wants you to forgive yourself.

> **God, be merciful to me because you are loving. Because you are always ready to be merciful, wipe out all my wrongs. Wash away all my guilt and make me clean again. I know about my wrongs, and I can't forget my sin. You are the only one I have sinned against; I have done what you say is wrong. . . . Take away my sin, and I will be clean. Wash me, and I will be whiter than snow. . . . Create in me a pure heart, God, and make my spirit right again. . . . You are not pleased by sacrifices,**

or I would give them. You don't want burnt
offerings. The sacrifice God wants is a broken
spirit. God, you will not reject a heart that is
broken and sorry for sin.

Ps. 51:1–4, 7, 10, 16–17

What Does God Do When We Sin?

Psalm 51 was written by King David. It was his
prayer of confession after some truly horrible sins. It
began when he had sex with Bathsheba, who was married to another man. But it didn't end there. She became
pregnant. He then arranged to have her husband killed
so no one would know that David was the real father.

Whatever sexual sin you may be guilty of, I doubt if
it's as horrible as David's. Yet he still came to God asking
for forgiveness, and God completely forgave him.

Here's a story that may hit a little closer to home. I
talked to a girl named Marsha one Sunday night on
DAWSON McALLISTER LIVE! She's nineteen, unmar-
ried, and has had a baby—not an ideal situation. But
Marsha's problems were more severe. Her pregnancy
had complications. Doctors said this was the only baby
she'd ever have.

Marsha was crushed and full of guilt. She was
convinced that she was being punished by God because
she had ignored His commands about premarital sex.

Marsha needed a new understanding of God's love
and forgiveness. True, she was facing some very painful
circumstances. But those were the terrible consequences

of her sin, not punishments from God. If you play with fire, you're gonna get burned. That's not a punishment; it's a consequence.

God doesn't just sit on His throne in heaven and plan ways to punish us for our sins. If that were His plan, He never would have brought Jesus Christ into the world to die for our sins. Jesus, who was innocent, brought the awful punishment of torture and death upon Himself so that we, who are guilty, could escape it and live in peace with God forever.

So what does God do when we sin? Does He take away the consequences? No, He doesn't. But He does cry with us. He hurts with us. And more than anything, He wants us to come to Him and ask for forgiveness.

So what happens when we ask God for forgiveness? When you say, "God, forgive me," what does He do? The Bible tells us this:

I will forgive them for the wicked things they did, and I will not remember their sins anymore.
Jer. 31:34b

In other words, God doesn't just forgive our sins, He completely forgets them. That's incredible.

If you have blown it sexually (or messed up any other way) and never asked God to forgive you, do it *now*. You may want to use the verses from Psalm 51 and Jeremiah 31 as your own personal prayer to God. Remember, God is gracious and loving. He is always ready to help us when we are humble enough to ask.

Once we have asked for forgiveness, do you know what happens next? He becomes merciful toward us. King David committed adultery with Bathsheba, then murdered her husband. Yet in Psalm 51:1 he was still able to pray,

God, be merciful to me because you are loving. Because you are always ready to be merciful, wipe out all my wrongs.

The word *merciful* in this verse means that God is willing and able to help us face the consequences of our sin. In fact, He begins to give us healing from the pain of our consequences the moment we confess.

The moment Marsha asked God to forgive her for having sex before marriage, He began to heal her heartbreak and help her face the natural consequences of her sin. God became totally focused on helping Marsha deal with her new baby and the complications of her pregnancy so she could get on with her life. Why? Because He loves her. AND HE LOVES YOU TOO!

Forgiving Yourself

There is one more issue you may need to deal with. You've made the commitment to be sexually pure from this point on. You've asked God to forgive you and He has. Yet you still feel guilty, even though you know you have honestly and sincerely confessed your sin to God. Why is this?

All sin, but especially sexual sin, can leave a deep scar on your emotions. It can be very difficult for you to forgive yourself. Satan knows this too. And he knows that the guiltier you feel the less effective you will be as a Christian. So he will constantly try to remind you that you have failed God and yourself. In fact, Revelation 12:10 calls Satan **"the accuser of our brothers and sisters."**

Once you have confessed your sin to God, you must trust what the Bible says, trust that God has both forgiven and forgotten your sins—FOREVER! When you choose to feel guilty and unforgiven, you are actually saying to God that your opinion is more important than His.

So if you have already confessed but are still feeling guilty, look again at the truth of Jeremiah 31:34:

> **I will forgive them for the wicked things they did, and I will not remember their sins anymore.**

Don't fall into Satan's trap by simply believing what you feel. Instead, put your faith into what God says in the Bible. He has never lied and He never will. God wants you to know that He now sees you as a virgin again. That's right. In His healing eyes you are a pure and holy virgin who is totally loved. And you have a great future because God Himself is planning it.

17

Love Worth Waiting For

*I will know I am developing
God's kind of loving
relationship when . . .
I am willing to wait for Him
to send me a godly dating
relationship.*

OK, DAWSON, SO WHAT DOES THIS BOOK HAVE TO DO WITH ME? I don't have a date. I don't have anybody. And the way things are going so far, I'm not sure I ever will."

I'm sure some of you probably feel that way right now. In fact, I'm convinced that nearly every student has felt this way at one time or another. Of course, I'm sure that doesn't make you feel much better about your situation. And I understand that. All of us want to be loved.

I hope you understand that God knows that too. After all, He made you that way. Your need for love was built in by God Himself. So don't get discouraged yet. God has every intention of helping you meet your need to be loved.

Here's part of a letter from a young girl who is struggling with loneliness because she doesn't have someone special to love her:

> So here's my story: For quite a while, I'd been praying for a boyfriend—not really for a romantic relationship, but just for someone to be a friend and help me overcome my loneliness.

> Every time I saw a young, happy couple some-
> where, I didn't get jealous but I felt lonely inside.
> Actually, I felt happy for them because I know
> what it's like to not have anybody to go to.
>   And I'm not a bit angry at God for not send-
> ing me someone. But I'm still waiting and trusting
> God to send me the guy He wants me to have.

Now here's a girl who is trying to see her life from God's perspective. Yes, she is lonely, but she is still trusting God to meet her relationship needs.

Why Don't I Have a Boyfriend or Girlfriend?

Let me encourage you to trust God's plan for your life. He knows exactly what you need and what you don't need. Let's take a look at several possible reasons why now may not be the right time for a boyfriend or girlfriend in your life.

Reason one: God wants you to learn to depend more on Him.

Sometimes students believe if they could only find the "right" guy or the "right" girl, all their problems would be solved. Then you would be totally happy, right? I know adults who are older than I am who still believe this. Let me tell you why it's not true. God never intended for us to depend upon a relationship with another person to meet the needs that only a relation-ship with Jesus Christ can fill.

Do you know one of the biggest reasons why there are so many divorces? It's because couples really think that after they are married, they will be able to meet all of each other's needs. BIG MISTAKE!

In fact, it's more than a mistake; it's a lie that Satan uses to trick us into not depending on God the way we should. And man, has it worked! It's left us with broken promises, broken homes, and broken families.

God wants to protect us from this lie. He wants us to keep our promises of love and build up our homes and cherish our families. But He wants us to understand that no matter how much we may one day love another person, only He can meet our deepest needs for love and acceptance.

Psalm 37:4 tells us to

Delight yourself in the LORD and he will give you the desires of your heart. (NIV)

Hey, the dating game can be overrated, but you can never run out of God's love. Tell Him you trust Him. He won't let you down.

Reason two: God wants you to get to know Him even better.

In Matthew 6:33 Jesus was talking to large crowd of people. This is what He told them:

The thing you should want most is God's kingdom and doing what God wants. Then all these other things you need will be given to you.

158

Notice that He didn't say, "The thing you should want most is a good date life," or "to be loved." No, God wants us to get to know Him like never before. He wants us to spend our time learning what pleases Him and then doing it. When we do that, He promises He will give us *everything*—not some things, but *everything* we need.

Reason three: God wants you to learn how to be a real servant.

The biggest surprise in most dating relationships is that they require a lot more giving than receiving. God wants you to learn how to be servants before an important relationship comes along. In fact, the Bible tells us that serving others is the real key to greatness:

> **Whoever wants to become great among you must serve the rest of you like a servant. Whoever wants to become first among you must serve the rest of you like a slave. In the same way, the Son of Man did not come to be served. He came to serve others and to give his life as a ransom for many people.**
>
> **Matt. 20:26–28**

God wants you to form friendships with lots of people, including those of the opposite sex. He doesn't want these friendships to be based on romance. He wants them to be based on service. Rather than feeling sorry for yourself because you aren't seeing someone special right now, try looking at people through the eyes of Jesus. He sees everyone as special. He wants you to have the pleasure of learning to give now. Becoming a true servant will prepare you to be a great dating partner.

Now You Know . . .

No matter how long it takes, don't make the mistake of thinking God has forgotten about you. God may seem slow—but He's always on time! It's hard to be patient, but it's even harder to get over a relationship that you weren't ready for.

God doesn't always give us what we'd like, but we're sure to like what He gives. And what He wants to give us is a perfect love life. And I promise you, when you know you're really in love, it'll be love that's worth waiting for!